THE ANTS

the ants

by Wilhelm Goetsch

ANN ARBOR

THE UNIVERSITY OF MICHIGAN PRESS

Preface

We have all had some dealings with ants. We may have thrust our spade into a swarm of them, or seen their columns on a tree or bush. They may have gotten into our sugar. Or we may have seen an anthill out in the country. How do these little animals live and work?

From time immemorial, ant communities have aroused interest and admiration. Herodotus reports that ants dragged grains of gold from deep in the earth. And Solomon says in his Proverbs: "Go to the ant, thou sluggard; consider her ways and be wise: which having no guide, overseer or ruler, provideth her meat in the summer, and gathereth her food in the harvest."

Once we study the ants more closely, we soon grow a little weary of such wonder and morality tales and reject impatiently any interpretation that deals with the ants as if they were little men. In fact, modern entomologists have thus rejected many observations of the ancients which ultimately turned out to be sound. Solomon, we shall see, was perfectly right in speaking of harvester ants, and Herodotus' story is not as farfetched as we had thought.

I was drawn to the study of ants partly by a desire to find out how much truth there was in the old legends. At first, I took it up as a pastime. But in my travels, I became more and more fascinated by the infinite variety of ant life. And the study of their social activities, their co-operative labors, has given me no end of delight.

My thanks are due to all the myrmecologists who were

my teachers and advisers, and to all my friends among colleagues and students. Though I seldom mention them by name, I shall draw amply on their findings.

It goes without saying that this little book represents no more than a small sampling of ant lore. An exhaustive work on the numerous varieties of ants and their societies would require many volumes.

W. Goetsch

Contents

THE ANTS

The Ant's Body

"The anthill," says the poet, *"is all abustle."* This simple statement of fact, without pedantry or romanticism, may well serve as a beginning for our study. We shall try to find out exactly what it is that bustles in an ant community.

Pick out a few ants from the familiar mound of the wood ant or from the nest of the little black garden ant. Ants taken from one colony look almost identical, though they may differ in size. But members of different colonies often differ slightly in color as well as in form. This fact alone tells us that we have no right to speak of *the* ant—there are a great many different species of ants. Each species breaks down into a number of subspecies and varieties, some 6,000 of which are known to us to day. To mention only one feature, some kinds of ants are one inch and others as small as one-twenty-fifth of an inch in length.

The body of the ant is divided into three segments, which can be distinguished with the naked eye in all but the very small varieties. The *head* is connected by a thin neck with the *thorax*, which in turn is connected by a "waist" with the *abdomen* (Fig. 1).

This body structure, with some variations, is found in all insects—in butterflies, beetles, dragonflies, and so on. It has proved extremely practical and efficient: more than three-quarters of all known animal species are insects. Insects have established themselves in all continental regions of the earth, and have shown themselves

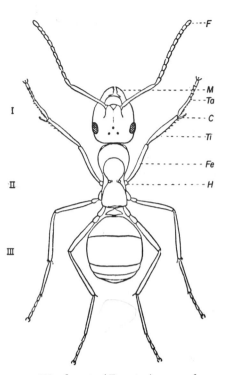

FIG. 1. Wood ant (*Formica*) seen from above. I. Head with antennae, or feelers (F), which consist of a shaft or scape in one piece and several short joints; upper mandible (M); two large compound eyes on the sides and three simple eyes on the forehead (these do not occur in all ants). II. Thorax with three pairs of legs, which consist of hip (H), femur (Fe), and tibia (Ti), and of the tarsal joints (Ta); C = cleaning apparatus. III. Abdomen, connected with the thorax by a stem or pedicel of one segment.

superior to almost all other organisms. They are inferior only to the vertebrates, and that chiefly in size.

Insects, including the ants, do not possess an inside

skeleton as we do, but have instead an outer armor. That is why they are hard to the touch. Their armor does not, like our skeleton, consist of bones; it is composed of a light yet very firm substance called chitin, which is secreted by the outer skin. Mobility is preserved by joints in the skin skeleton. The joints of the ant show the most minute articulation down to the last member, and especially between the main parts of its body—the head, the thorax, and the abdomen.

The head is the seat of the sense organs and of the higher "mental" faculties—a fitting term, as we shall often have occasion to point out. The most striking features of the head are the antennae or feelers (Fig. 1); they are long and extremely mobile, and consist of a scape, or shaft, in one single joint, and a funiculus, or lash, made up of nine to thirteen joints. The funiculus is normally somewhat thicker at the tip, to make room for the organs of touch and smell, which are most abundant there. For example, 211 olfactory cones and 1,730 touch bristles have been counted on a single antenna of the wood ant. Even this figure is conservative. Other ants, which lack the good eyesight of the wood ant—as for example one of the blind South American legionary ants (*Eciton mars*) —have a much larger number.

The ant's antennae are always in motion. An ant can do something that is utterly beyond us: it can feel objects from all sides and smell them at the same time. In this way it perceives round, square, hard, and soft smells, just as we gain an impression of both shape and texture by touching and looking at an object at the same time.

The other sensory organs are much less important than the versatile antennae. The head often has extremely large eyes, to be sure, of the form usual in insects: they are composed of many minute separate eyes (facets), each of which produces not a complete image, but only a point. To get some idea of what this is like, you only need to look through a magnifying glass at a newspaper reproduction of a photograph; the image will break up into many dots. Television, too, is based on a succession of such dots. But we do not find such compound eyes in all ants. Some forms of ants are totally blind, though they still find their way around quite well, and between the sharp-sighted and the blind ants there are all sorts of

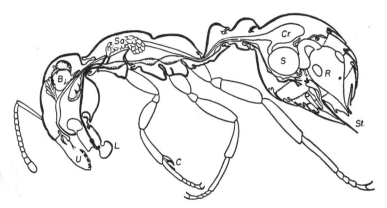

FIG. 2. Side view of the hunter ant (*Myrmica*). U = upper mandible, L = lower mandible with tongue, B = brain, Sa = salivary gland, Cr = crop, S = stomach, R = rectum with adjacent glands, St = sting, C = cleaning mechanism on the first leg. In this genus the abdomen is connected with the thorax by a pedicel of two segments.

intermediate stages. Some species also have small, simple eyespots or ocelli in addition to the large lateral eyes. Because of their position these eyespots, which come in threes, are also called frontal eyes (Fig. 1).

All the sense organs are connected with the brain by nerve fibers. The pedunculate organs—white bands—of the brain are the source of higher mental faculties of the ants, which enable them to perform their varied social operations (Fig. 3).

Next we come to the mouth parts, most important of which are the jaws (mandibles). The mandibles do not transmit sense impressions, but they have many other uses. They are usually shovel-shaped, with pointed tooth-like protuberances on the exposed edge. This edge has been called, incorrectly, the chewing edge—the little

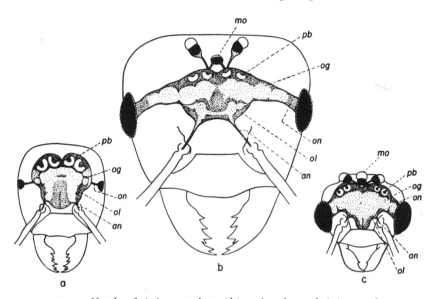

FIG. 3. Heads of (*a*) a worker, (*b*) a female, and (*c*) a male, of a garden ant (*Lasius*): mo = median ocellus, pb = pedunculate bodies corresponding to the cerebrum of the vertebrates, og = optic ganglion, on = optic nerve, ol = olfactory lobe, an = antennary nerve.

teeth do not serve for cutting up food, but for carrying building material, digging and building, grasping and dismembering enemies or prey, and many other purposes. The ant uses his jaws as we use our hands. In the lower jaws are situated taste organs and special appendages that often look like feelers. Here also is a bristly comb, with which the ant cleans its long antennae, combing off all foreign substances. When an ant finds itself in strange surroundings it will comb away at its antennae at great length, like an old scholar wiping his glasses before getting down to work.

The edges of the secondary jaws serve for chewing, but their action is totally different from that of our jaws. We bite from up to down and crush the food by a sidewise movement, but the ant's jaws move against each other from left to right. Since the chewing surfaces are thin and fine, ants as a rule can consume only very soft food.

The so-called tongue (Fig. 2), attached to the lower lip, is a highly developed organ. It serves not only for taking in food but also for cleaning. When an ant is at rest it is always licking at one thing or another—its companions, its larvae, or its pupae.

The ant's head also contains salivary glands, some of which reach as far down as the thorax (Fig. 2). When the ant chews, the secretions of these glands come out in large drops and work on the food before it enters the mouth; grains of starch, for example, are turned into sugar—a process which in human beings the saliva performs in the mouth. The ant also uses the secretion of these glands to feed its young. From the mouth the food enters the foregut, which passes through the thorax. No further digestion of food takes place here, for the thorax serves only to anchor the three pairs of legs (Fig. 1), which are attached to the thoracic rings by the hip joint (coxa) and the trochanter. The leg is divided into two parts: the upper thigh (femur) and the lower shank (tibia). At the end of the legs are the feet (tarsi), each of which bears a pair of tiny claws. The first pair of legs also has two little combs set side by side. The ant draws its antennae between these two combs to clean them (Figs. 1 and 2).

Some ants also have wings; these ants will be discussed later.

The last part of the ant's body is the abdomen, where digestion takes place. As the food leaves the foregut it passes first of all into the crop (Fig. 2). The crop is a kind of elastic bladder which the ant stuffs as full as possible. To say that a man stuffs himself is to accuse him of selfishness and gluttony. With the ants exactly the opposite is true; for what goes into the crop is intended not for the individual but for the community. From this "social stomach," as the crop is called, the food is vomited up and shared with other ants. A simple experiment will show how this happens. When honey or sugar water is dyed blue and fed to an ant, the color shows through the ant's abdomen. Shortly after an ant marked in this way has gone back to its nest, many of its companions have similarly colored bellies. These ants have been fed by the first.

This social stomach is entirely separate from the ant's real stomach. Before it can digest any of the food, the ant must pump the food out of the crop into the real stomach.

When the crop is full, the abdomen can readily be examined from outside. It is composed of a number of rings, which are in turn divided into back and belly plates. The membranes between the plates are extremely flexible, so that when the crop is filled the plates are forced apart. When the abdomen is less full, the plates overlap and are harder to distinguish.

The pedicel—the movable link between abdomen and thorax—may be considered a part of the abdomen. In the subfamily Formicinae (Fig. 1), the pedicel consists of one piece; in the subfamily Myrmicinae (Fig. 2), of two pieces.

Besides the digestive organs the abdomen also contains a device for releasing poison. This device varies considerably from subfamily to subfamily. Some (Myrmicinae, Fig. 2) have a real stinger like a bee's, with which they can inflict considerable pain. The sting releases a poison in the wound, and the victim feels a painful burning for a long time. The more familiar varieties (Formicinae) have a poison bladder instead of a stinger; these ants first bite their enemy and then squirt their poison into the bite. By raising the tip of their abdomen they can also squirt drops of poison for an impressive distance. You can test this for yourself. Stir up a colony of wood ants, and then hold a cloth at some distance from them. You will find that the cloth soon smells strongly of acid.

The abdomen is also the seat of the sexual glands. In this respect, however, most ants are very poorly supplied. If you look very closely you will sometimes find that the ant has atrophied ovaries, which seldom contain eggs that can be laid. As we shall see in the next section, these ants are females that have not developed fully. They may be large or small, for a small ant is not always a young one and a large one is not necessarily mature.

Eggs, Larvae, and Pupae

Ant eggs are very tiny. From them emerge the larvae, legless "grubs" like the larvae of flies (Fig. 5). These larvae are cared for by the grown ants, who give them liquid food from the crop as well as solid morsels. In time the larvae grow into pupae. Some forms of ant first spin themselves into a cocoon, after the manner of butterfly caterpillars or silkworms. The pupae wrapped in such cocoons are sold as "ants' eggs" and used as food for birds or fishes.

Not all pupae have cocoons; many varieties of ant produce cocoonless pupae, in which the form of the future ant can be clearly seen (Fig. 5 b). After a certain period of rest the ant slips out fully grown, having completed its growth in the period between egg and pupa.

Who lays these eggs, around which the bustling activity of the ant colony revolves? Our next section will be devoted to this question.

Castes and Classes

All the eggs of a colony are laid by one ant, the so-called "queen"; she is the mother of the whole nest and is usually the only fully developed female in it. In some species she is distinguished by her enormous size (Fig. 7); in others she is not much larger than her companions (Fig. 4 a). But distinguishing marks can always be found on the three main parts of her body.

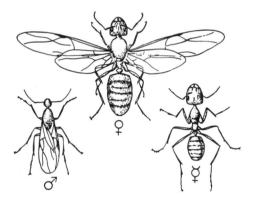

FIG. 4 a. Castes of the carpenter ant (*Camponotus herculaneus*). The male ♂ (lives only a short time and dies after fertilization). Winged female ♀ (after fertilization casts off wings and becomes queen of the colony, cf. Fig. 4 b). Worker (large form).

The queen's head has three simple eyespots in addition to the two large compound eyes, and her antennae are often more sensitive than those of the workers. On the other hand, those parts of her brain that serve the higher mental functions are less developed (Fig. 3). The queen's thorax is arched, and remnants of wings can be recognized, for the queen, as we shall soon see, originally had wings (Figs. 4 *a* and 7 *b*). The abdomen may also be extremely large. The sexual glands, which take up most of the room, are often so enormous that they distend the

FIG. 4 *b*. Queen who has shed her wings, with brood (eggs and young larvae).

plates. A queen's performance is often extraordinary; some queens can lay eggs every few minutes, thus becoming the mother of a whole colony; for all the creatures we see bustling about the anthill are the offspring of one queen or at most of a very few queens.

The mass of the citizens in the ant society are the so-called workers. They too are females, but their growth is stunted; they almost always lack the essential feature of womanhood, the power to reproduce. Their sexual glands are either deficient or wholly absent. But their feminine instincts are fully developed, and with the utmost devotion they care for the eggs, larvae, and pupae produced by the queen. Since the care of the children requires these stunted females to get food and build dwellings, they have been given the name of workers. The activity of these workers and their astonishing division of labor have led to comparison between ant societies and human societies, but the comparison should not be carried too far. No human queen ever populated a whole state with her offspring, or ruled over a society composed of sexless female servants.

The so-called soldiers, a special category of workers, are also females. Most soldiers have enormous heads with

a

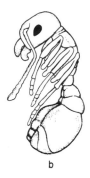

b

FIGS. 5 *a* and 5 *b*. *a*) Brood of the Italian house ant, *Pheidole pallidula*. To the left, larvae of varying ages, and a pupa lying on its back; to the right, a large larva eating a crumb of food (part of an insect's larva). *b*) Pupa of *Pheidole* more powerfully magnified.

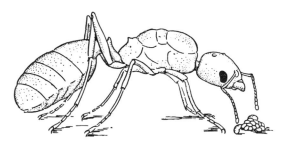

FIG. 6. Young queen of the Italian house ant (*Pheidole pallidula*), who has shed her wings, with her first eggs and two larvae.

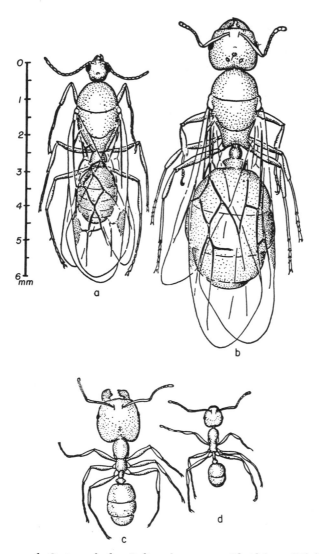

FIG. 7 a-d. Castes of the Italian house ant *Pheidole pallidula*.
a) Winged male. b) Winged female, who after shedding her wings
becomes a queen (cf. Fig. 6). c) Special form of stunted female,
representing a small minority of the population (= soldier).
d) Stunted female of the sort that forms the bulk of the population
(= worker).

powerful mandibles. The differences between a common worker and a soldier can be seen in Figs. 7 and 8. Fig. 7 *c-d* shows a soldier and a worker of the Italian house ant (*Pheidole pallidula*) equally magnified. Fig. 8 shows heads of each of the two castes.

Misled by the name of soldier, some people suppose that these big-heads are particularly warlike. Actually, they are remarkable chiefly as defenders of the home. With its thick skull, which is protected by a hard skin as though by a steel helmet, a soldier will often block the whole entrance to the nest, so that intruders cannot get in. In one variety (*Colobopsis truncata*, Fig. 22), which occurs in Europe, the head of the soldier is especially adapted for this blockade; it looks like a stopper. This ant makes its nest in branches, and the soldiers cork up the little entrance holes simply by sticking their heads into them.

The soldiers are not, however, particularly aggressive; as warriors they are far outdone by the simple workers. Among meat-eating ants, the workers usually attack the prey or enemies; the soldiers appear only later. Then, to be sure, the soldiers' powerful mandibles are put to good use; they dig in like bulldogs, and the victim is quickly torn into little bits which are carried off by the workers. The soldiers do not take part in the work of carrying the

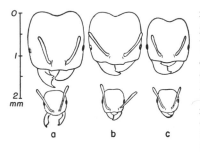

FIG. 8 *a-c*. Heads of soldiers and workers of the Italian house ant *Pheidole pallidula* (cf. Fig. 7), from different colonies. *a*) Naples, Zoological Station. *b*) Torbole on Lake Garda. *c*) Naples, Posilippo; smallest soldier so far measured. As in many other drawings, only the shafts of the antennae are shown; the funiculi (lashes) are omitted.

food home, and for this reason it was formerly supposed that they did no work in the nest. It has been discovered, however, that the soldiers of *Pheidole* and *Colobopsis* often take part in the care of the brood; they lick the larvae and carry them about with loving care, demonstrating the primary importance in their lives of the maternal instinct.

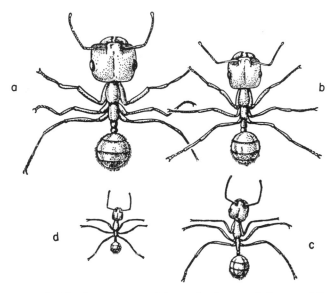

FIG. 9 *a-d* The harvester ant *Messor barbarus*. *a*) Large soldier. *b*) Average-sized soldier. *c*) Intermediate form. *d*) Small worker.

In many varieties of ants the gap between worker and soldier is filled in by intermediate types; every stage can be found, from "giants," or supersoldiers, to average-sized soldiers, and from pygmy soldiers to undersized workers. These gradations are most readily observed among the harvester ants (Fig. 9) and the fungus growers (Fig. 36), of which we shall speak later. Among these ants there is usually a special division of labor: the smaller workers are ordinarily occupied at home, while the larger ones are engaged in outside activities.

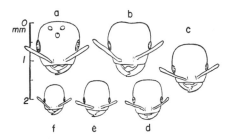

FIG. 10 *a-f.* Heads of different castes of the Chilean ant *Solenopsis gayi. a*) Female with three frontal eyes. *b*) Giant (= a soldier attaining the size of a queen). *c-e*) Transitional forms. *f*) Smallest worker.

Transitional forms between workers or soldiers and genuine females are also found. The giants show some resemblance to the queens in the structure of their eyes and brain, and they sometimes attain the size of queens. Here we have one more indication of the relationship between the workers and soldiers and the true females.

Among this multitude of females the males appear only at certain times. As a rule they are smaller than the females (Figs. 3 and 7), and have smaller brains (Fig. 3). Their eyes, however, are larger than those of their nest mates, and their organs of smell are more sensitive, making it easier for them to find the female. Their whole existence is "attuned to love"; this is their only world. They appear for the sole purpose of fertilizing a few young females and never take part in the work of the colony.

A Colony Is Founded—
The Marriage Flight

This brings us to an important point in the life of the ant: the establishment of new colonies.

A new colony is usually set up as a separate nest. At certain times a new group of queens and males is born among the workers in the old nest; both have wings (Figs. 4 and 7), and both fly from their native colony to mate high in the air. All the different ant varieties of a given region usually set off on these marriage flights at the same time; in every nest the winged males and females stand waiting impatiently for the stimulus that will release the flight. As a rule a fine warm day with sufficient dampness and perhaps a hint of storm in the air will set them off, like a coin inserted in a juke-box. Then the melody of new life begins; once the spring has been released, there is no stopping the foreordained chain of events. Everywhere the ants issue forth from the nests; even the wingless workers are infected by the excitement and accompany their brothers and sisters as far as they can, to nearby flower stems, clumps of vegetation, or high stones, from which the winged ones take off on their flight.

The number of ants in these swarms is sometimes almost unbelievable. Three thousand five hundred males and 35,000 females of a South American variety (*Atta*) were once observed in a single nest.

Such mass flights are also seen beside the Mediterranean. At Punta Tragara, one of the loveliest spots in Capri

(Fig. 79), I once observed a marriage flight which presented a profound spectacle of birth and death in nature. As the sun went down, the Italian house ants (*Pheidole pallidula*) began to swarm. From all sides appeared bands of the little winged males; these bands quickly joined to form a light cloud which danced up and down over the blue seashore for the brief moment which was both the climax and the end of their lives.

Then came the much larger females. They rose heavily into the air; their wings are smaller than those of the males, and their movement was slowed by the masses of eggs they carried. At first the females flew about singly, but as soon as they noticed the swarm of males they hurried into its midst. Wherever the females appeared, a wild movement began. The males dashed headlong toward them; a mad whirl, and a male had achieved his purpose. Joined together, male and female fell zigzagging to the ground, where after a short time the fertilization process was completed.

With fertilization the male's destiny is accomplished; he has filled the female's seed bag and supplied her with sperm for the rest of her life. The male who has mated dies immediately after the marriage flight, while his less fortunate companions soon languish away.

Even during the marriage flight itself death lurked in wait: with a shrill scream the terns darted down at the descending couples; a snap of the bill and all was over.

When German ants mate they usually fly to high places —mountain tops, solitary trees, weathercocks, or observation towers—and the swarms are sometimes so dense than they look like rising smoke. People have actually called the fire department on such occasions.

The mating of winged ants from different colonies is biologically important because it reduces inbreeding. But we find in these meetings another example of the lavish wastefulness of nature. I once found the floor of an observation tower in the Black Forest covered with a half-inch layer of dead males of many different species.

For the females who have escaped from the perils of the marriage flight, the routine of life continues. They fall to the ground and attempt to hide; for again grave dangers surround them. All the birds and animals that eat ants—and in tropical South America this includes even man—are ready to pounce on the fat morsels. Only a very few females escape to begin the next chapter of their life story.

The next move seems very odd. The females bend over sideways and press their bodies to the ground or against stones, stretching their wings in a peculiar way in order to break them off. As a rule the wing breaks off easily. If the ant does not succeed, however, the wings shrink little by little and are shed piecemeal, for soon after the marriage flight the flight muscles and wing tissues begin to shrivel up. This process takes place after a certain time even in individuals that have not been fertilized.

Once she has lost her wings the fertilized female becomes a queen and begins to search for a suitable place to build her future colony.

The various kinds of ants build their nests in different ways: the tree dwellers gnaw a hollow in rotten wood, the earth ants dig into the ground or crawl under stones. In each case, however, the queen builds a closed chamber in which she seals herself off from the outside world. For her own protection and that of the future colony she must remain incommunicado, going without food until the first workers develop from the eggs that she now begins to lay. Since the development of the young takes some time—in southern ants about four weeks and in our northern varieties nine months or more—the queen undergoes a long fast.

The queen's fast is relieved in two ways. First, she has

an inner source of nourishment in the useless wing muscles which occupy almost her entire thorax. Little by little the muscles disappear; the fibers shrink, and the substances released are used to nourish the queen and her eggs. In this way the useless muscles perform the function of a storehouse, very much as does the hump of a camel. In addition, only 10 to 20 per cent of the eggs the queen lays develop into larvae; the rest are eaten.

Even this food does not all go to the queen; she must also raise her brood. In order to get a working force as quickly as possible, the queen ant has developed a peculiar habit: when a few larvae have emerged from the eggs, she chooses the largest and gives it the largest part of the food. As a result it quickly grows into a pupa. The next share of food goes to the second largest larva, and so on, so that at first only a few larvae mature very quickly. When a force of workers has developed, they treat the larvae in the same way.

The first workers to emerge are usually smaller than the later ones will be. These minims serve to relieve their mother; they devote themselves to the care of the new brood, and after a few days they begin to bore through the cell walls and venture into the world. In their first labors the young ants remind us of playful puppies. They do not know quite what to do when they find their first prey, a fly or other small insect. Soon, however, they overcome their fear and indecision, take the prey, and drag it into the nest.

With the arrival of the first prey, or in some species when the first liquid food is brought into the nest, a new phase begins for the colony. The larvae, still pale from feeding on their mother's eggs, suddenly take on a new color; one can see their bodies filled with the food that the little workers have brought from outside, and even the reddish yellow honey or chewed-up flies they have eaten. Their little stomachs are filled to bursting, and the contents shine clearly through the whitish skin (cf. Fig. 5).

We now leave the larvae to their own resources and turn for a moment to their nurses, the small workers. In some varieties the small workers have a very brief life span. This clearly distinguishes them from the larger workers, who live at least six months.

The first workers are nevertheless extremely important in the building of the colony. Their small size does not prevent them from performing the necessary tasks of child-raising, building, and food gathering, and the shortness of their life makes no difference to the new community. During their lifetime the larvae of later, better-nourished eggs grow up, so that when the small workers die new and stronger companions are ready to take their place.

In some colonies the second series also consists of small workers, though even within one species slight differences may occur. If this series includes soldiers, the new colony is complete.

The type of colony formation just described is the usual one. The old colony discharges male and female germs as a plant does its pollen, and once the queen is fertilized she becomes the seed of the new organism. Like the promiscuous strewing of seeds, this process is extremely wasteful. Such waste is, however, absolutely necessary, since it is only by chance that any of the queens survive. As a result, the ants sometimes use a less perilous method of colonization.

Parasitic colony formation, although it avoids the perils of independent colony formation, involves still other dangers. The young female, immediately after the marriage flight, is received by a colony that already has a queen but is large enough for the queens to live separately. Such colonies occur frequently, even in species capable of independent colony formation. A subspecies of the large reddish brown ant (*Formica rufa*) presents such a case. If the communicating passages between the pine-needle mounds of the nest are destroyed, new independent colonies may come into being.

Sometimes the marriage flight is dispensed with altogether, and the queen is fertilized at home, but this involves the danger of inbreeding. Joining another colony, however, also involves dangers. Like all monarchs the queens are jealous, and as a rule they tolerate no rivals. When two queens meet they almost always fight, and such battles are gruesome to behold. No quarter is given. Each contestant tries to seize the other by the neck and as soon as one succeeds she saws off her rival's head.

The workers are often hostile to newly arrived queens. As a rule a queen is welcomed into a strange nest only if the old queen has died. Then the workers are friendly; they begin at once to lick and caress the new queen as though indulging in a pleasure of which they had long been deprived. The source of their delight is probably the sweet smell and taste of the stuff she exudes; and this too explains why the queens of alien species are regularly taken in by certain ants. For example, fertilized females of the jet-black ant (*Lasius fuliginosus*) are regularly taken into the queenless nests of related species (*Lasius bruneus*, and so forth); with her hosts the queen carries out the first step in colony formation. The original inhabitants of the nest, the so-called auxiliaries, later die out, and since only one queen is present to provide new progeny the colony gradually becomes pure-blooded.

Another kind of parasitic colony formation is practiced by the warlike blood-red ant (*Formica sanguinea*). The queen finds a colony that has no queen of its own and attacks the workers from ambush, stabbing them one by one. She then carries off the pupae and raises them to be her slaves, thus sparing herself the long wait until her own first workers grow up. Since the newborn ants know nothing of what has happened, they treat the strange queen as their own: they care for her eggs and bring up the young workers as if they were their own kin.

Such a colony, made up of several varieties of ants, is called a compound nest. The helper ants are usually called slaves, although they are neither oppressed nor forced to labor. They live exactly as they would in their own colony and are called slaves only because they were kidnapped from their original nests.

The workers of the blood-red ant are as fierce as the queen. Large troops of them invade the nests of other ants and kidnap the pupae, which they either eat immediately or store away for food. If the pupae belong to certain closely related species, however, the invaders carry them off to their own nest to add to the number of helpers. The colonies of the blood-red ant are almost always of the compound type.

The blood-red ant can, if necessary, carry on all the functions of the colony without helpers. But another variety, the Amazon ant (*Polyergus rufescens*), has so accustomed itself to the use of slaves that it cannot live without them. Its mandibles have developed into a terrible, dagger-like weapon, a single bite of which suffices to dispatch an enemy ant. But as the jaws developed into weapons they lost their usefulness for other purposes, and can no longer be used to break up food. As a result these warlike ants cannot even eat by themselves, but must be fed by their slaves.

If this development goes far enough, the relation between masters and slaves is reversed. As the jaws grow larger and larger they become useless even as weapons, and the original masters turn into parasites. There are many such ants leading an easy life in the nests of other species. In these parasitic colonies, as in parasitic individuals, only the essentials survive. One is reminded of certain of our intestinal worms in which almost the whole body structure disappears and only a reproductive organ is left. In species that have a soldier caste, this caste sometimes dwindles to the point of extinction. In others the soldiers are the first to be exterminated, as we shall see below. The workers dwindle and, in extreme cases, vanish completely leaving only the highly regressed females who because of their pleasant odors and secretions are allowed to live side by side with the queens and helpers. In this respect the parasite females are very much like certain other animals which the ants tolerate or even cultivate. Of these we shall speak in the next section.

Aliens and Enemies

In addition to its various castes an ant colony always includes numerous other boarders. Some, which live only on the surface, can be dangerous enemies; there may be spiders who feed on their hosts or certain ichneumons that lay their eggs in the nest, or beetles that raid the nest and steal the young ants. For the present, however, we shall turn to the parasites that live with the ants inside the nest.

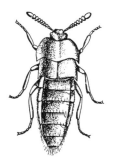

FIG. 11. Small beetle of the genus *Dinarda*. Tolerated in ants' nests because its great mobility makes it hard to attack. (After Wheeler.)

The underground yellow ant *Lasius flavus* makes a little hill in a meadow at the edge of a forest. When we open one of these hills we find all sorts of creatures in the nest. First, near the entrance, we shall probably find a number of little insects resembling plant lice. These are aphids, of whom we shall have more to say later. Next we come across various uninvited guests—caterpillars, cockchafers, grubs, and worms—who once they have been discovered will be attacked as intruders. Various insect larvae, as well as certain wood lice which are so heavily armored that the ants cannot attack them, live permanently in the nest without being molested.

Along with the accidental visitors and tolerated aliens, we find the real "guests," the most interesting of which is the clavigerid beetle (*Claviger testaceus*, Fig. 12). These blind beetles fearlessly approach the ants and "court" them with their club-shaped feelers, asking for food with the same gesture the ants use. In response, the ant spits up a drop of food for the beetle. The beetle also has something to offer; from several glands opening on its back it secretes a sweetish liquid which the ants greedily lick up. Here we have a case of symbiosis, of two different animals living together for mutual advantage.

We find a somewhat different relationship between the blood-red ants (*Formica sanguinea*) and certain short-winged beetles (*Dinarda*, Fig. 11) which in their shape and color more or less resemble the ants. The beetle's black body and its truncated wing tops, which are reddish brown like the thorax of the ant, may deceive the ant into thinking that this is one of its fellows. Sometimes, however, the ants will attack. When this happens the beetles lie flat on the ground and after a few

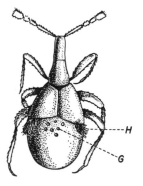

FIG. 12. Small beetle of the genus *Claviger*. Tolerated in ants' nests because of its secretions, which the ants like to lick up. When the hairs (H) are touched, the glands (G) begin to secrete.

FIG. 13. Tufted beetle *Atemeles*. Fed by the ants, in return it exudes at P a substance which the ants eagerly lick up. *Atemeles* is a "public enemy" which feeds on the brood of the ants.

FIG. 14 *a-b*. Beetle of the genus *Lomachusa* with larva (*b*). The same relation prevails between ant and beetle as with *Atemeles* (Fig. 13). Here the ants also care for the larvae of the "enemy of the state."

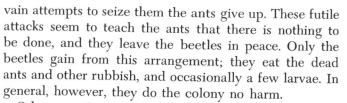

a   b

vain attempts to seize them the ants give up. These futile attacks seem to teach the ants that there is nothing to be done, and they leave the beetles in peace. Only the beetles gain from this arrangement; they eat the dead ants and other rubbish, and occasionally a few larvae. In general, however, they do the colony no harm.

Other parasites are more harmful. The blood-red ants have a particular enemy in a beetle of the genus *Lomachusa* (Fig. 14). This beetle, about one-fifth of an inch long, secretes from its hair a drug which the ants hold in high esteem. Because of their taste for this drug the ants feed and care for the beetles as they do their own queens and even care for the beetles' larvae, which do the colony no end of harm. The larvae feed on the colony's most precious possession, the brood. One egg after another is sucked out, one larva after another is eaten, and instead of putting a stop to the ravage the ants merely spit up drops of food for the beetle larvae. One explanation for the ants' behavior may be found in the fact that when the beetle larvae are hungry they act just as ant larvae do, wagging their heads back and forth until they are fed.

If the ants are lavish in their care of these beetle larvae, they are equally destructive of the pupae—but only by a strange and happy accident. When the beetle's larva is grown, the ants bed it down in a little hollow in the earth along with their own larvae. The ant larvae proceed to spin a thick cocoon, but the beetle larvae produce a very delicate one which is always damaged when the ants dig it out to move it. Seeing the damage, the ants pull out the larva and bury it again, compelling it to spin a new cocoon. This process so weakens the larva that it cannot pupate. As a result, only the *Lomachusa* larvae that the ants overlook can develop into beetles. By this strange misunderstanding the ant colony is preserved.

In cases of parasitism, we often find a remarkably favorable characteristic—such as the begging gesture of the beetle larvae—accompanied by another which largely annuls its effect. Without this precarious balance the relationship would be impossible. If, for example, the *Lomachusa* larvae were adapted to the ants' rough handling, the beetles would become so numerous that the blood-red ants would soon die out; in the end this would mean the downfall of the *Lomachusa*. In the course of the earth's history such relationships must often have been destroyed by fortunate accidents, while those marked by *imperfect* adaptation endured.

The *Lomachusa* beetles sometimes do enough damage to endanger the future of the ant colony. Wasmann and Forel, who have made a thorough study of the relationship, compare it to such human vices as addiction to alcohol or drugs. In each case society is damaged by the individual's craving for a substance that gives him pleasure. The ants, however, do not seem to tend the enemy brood with the conscious intent of later getting the drug; for when they are grown the *Lomachusa* beetles leave the nest of the blood-red ant and live for a time in other ant colonies.

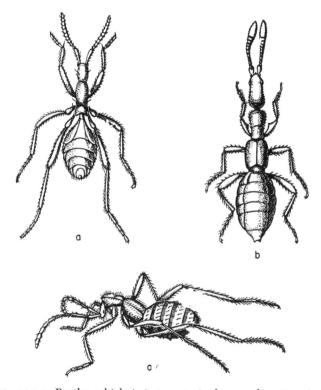

FIG. 15 *a-c*. Beetles which imitate ants in form and motion (ant apes). *a*) *Mimeciton pulex. b*) *Ecitomorpha simulans. c*) *Dorylostethus wasmanni.* (After Wheeler.) All these beetles live with the driver ants (Fig. 17).

These are only a few of the best-known instances of symbiosis between ants and other insects. The number of such relationships is legion, and almost every investigation of a little-known ant species yields a list of enemies and aliens who have adapted themselves to look like their hosts (Fig. 15). It would take a whole book to deal with them.

Warfare and Hunting

Most ant societies are organized for total warfare. The workers, which make up the mass of the population, become fighters when necessary, and the queen often takes part, at least when it comes to defending the nest. These are joined by the slower soldiers with their oversized weapons. Only the males are left out; since they possess neither poison gland nor stinger and their jaws are underdeveloped, they lack all aptitude for war, which is carried on by the female in these Amazonian societies.

Fighting goes on constantly in nearly all ant colonies, mostly in single combats. Battles are continuously in progress on the borders of the colonies, which include not only the nest but the nearby hunting grounds. Among ants, as among men, a strong state tries to spread out as much as possible and must keep defending its conquests.

Among the seed-gathering *Messor* ants, which we shall later examine more closely, we often find the borders guarded by sentinels. These ants assume a special position: the antennae are laid back, the legs are drawn close, and the whole body is pressed against the earth. This posture, in which the ants remain motionless for hours, has been called the sentinel's position, but we find ants in the same posture in the middle of the nest. At such times the ant is probably resting. Ants are not always hard at work; like bees, they often take long rests. An anthill always seems to be bustling because under natural conditions we cannot observe the animals that are resting. A *Messor* ant that is wandering around with nothing to do will assume the rest position if it comes upon a protected spot, such as a connecting passage in the nest (cf. Fig. 66). *Messor* ants also take up this position when they find themselves in an unfamiliar situation. A young ant emerging from the nest, already tired and afraid to venture out into the unknown, may stop to rest in this manner. When one ant sees another in this position, it too may sit down; whole congregations are formed in this way. The arrival of another ant may, however, induce a sitter to move on; if the newcomer happens to be tired, he will sit down in his turn. In this way one relays the other.

Ants sometimes rest in the open, usually at the edge of the hunting ground where the unknown begins. In this way the sentries form a ring around the hunting ground, but we need not assume that they are "consciously" guarding the area any more than are the ants that block the nest entrances by sitting down to rest in them.

In both instances the habit of the sentinel's position is useful to the community: the resting ants are on guard the moment anything out of the ordinary happens. The passage of a strange ant acts as a violent stimulus. The sentry thrusts her head forward, or may even leap at the enemy. Once the foe is seized, the assailant recoils swiftly without releasing her grip, drawing the enemy into her own territory; here she finishes it off with her jaws, her stinger, or the poison from her abdominal gland. Sometimes her fellows join in, and the fight becomes a mass battle.

The best way to observe one of these battles is to put members of different colonies into an artificial nest. The two parties spring wildly at one another spraying their poison, thrusting with their stingers, and trying to bite off one another's heads or abdomens. Even the severely wounded sometimes continue the battle. In one such battle two *Messor* ants whose abdomens had been entirely severed kept attacking their weary enemies after

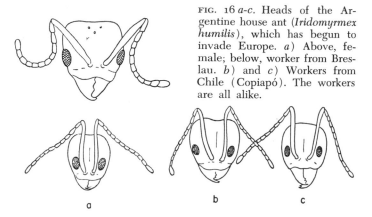

FIG. 16 *a-c.* Heads of the Argentine house ant (*Iridomyrmex humilis*), which has begun to invade Europe. *a*) Above, female; below, worker from Breslau. *b*) and *c*) Workers from Chile (Copiapó). The workers are all alike.

the other combatants had subsided in exhaustion and both parties had withdrawn into corners.

I once witnessed a violent battle when I put a few Argentine house ants (*Iridomyrmex humilis*, Fig. 16) into an artificial nest inhabited by a group of the Italian *Pheidole pallidula* (cf. Fig. 7). In the ensuing battle the two adversaries used entirely different techniques. The Italians, workers and soldiers at once, attacked furiously, gnashing wildly about like bulldogs, using no caution. The Argentines, on the other hand, never came close to the dangerous mandibles, but danced round their assailants like cautious boxers. Waiting for an unguarded spot, they would attack the enemy from the side or from behind and seize him by the leg. Once this was done, the Argentine pulled back and a second Argentine seized another leg. Now the Italian was done for; with its legs pulled in opposite directions, it was held fast, unable to use its own weapons. In a moment its legs were bitten off. All this happened in less time than you have taken to read the last three sentences. The Argentines with their treacherous effective tactics were always victorious, even against larger opponents such as wood ants.

The Argentine ant is now on a far-flung warpath. It is spreading all over the world, and wherever it shows up the native ants begin to disappear. Authorities now believe that *Iridomyrmex* originally migrated to Argentina from the warmer territories of Brazil and Bolivia. From Argentina it has embarked on its campaigns of conquest, making long journeys over the sea in shipments of fruits and plants. *Iridomyrmex* has no fixed nests, but sets up colonies wherever it can find food. The queens, who are wanderers too, soon join the new colonies, and so the breed spreads. This ant came to New Orleans in 1891, probably in a shipment of coffee, and soon spread as far as Tennessee, North Carolina, and Texas, where it became a familiar household pest. In the West it found a home in California, where its presence was first noted in 1907; I have found the breed in Copiapó, Chile, and other observers have seen it in Concepción.

The Argentine ant first appears in ports. In 1908, during the Boer War, it was brought to Cape Town in shipments of fodder; since that time it has made itself at home in all South Africa. In Teneriffe and other Canary Islands it lives in the open as well as in houses. From 1882 on the same sort of battles that took place in my artificial nest must have raged on a large scale in the Azores and Madeira, for since that date, when the Argentine ant was introduced, the *Pheidole* has disappeared from Madeira. In Lisbon and Oporto the battle is apparently still going on, but the Argentine ant is already in the majority. It has marched victoriously through Spain, southern France, and Bosnia, and in all these regions is found in the open as well as in houses. The same is true of Naples and its environs, where I first noted its presence in 1936. It has recently conquered the islands of Capri, Ischia, and Majorca (1953).

Wherever it cannot live in the open all year, the Argentine ant invades houses; it has been reported in Brussels, in Paris, where a hotel once had to be evacuated on its account, in Berlin, and most recently in Hamburg. In the Breslau Botanical Gardens it has become a serious nuisance.

Why does the Argentine ant attract such attention as a household pest? First of all, it multiplies at a stupendous rate. Between April and September one colony grew from a population of 100 to 10,000. The ants invade a house en masse and get into everything, even into the beds. They attack every conceivable human foodstuff. From the highest attic to the deepest cellar nothing edible is safe from them, and it is useless to set food in water, because the Argentine ants swim right through it. They are particularly fond of sweets; one swarm emptied a jar of jam in a few hours. They also enjoy meat and are quite capable of attacking young birds in the nest and little chickens in the coop. The fact that they do away with all vermin and leave no bugs of any sort alive is but feeble consolation.

The wars of the Argentine ant, as of other species, turn out to be large-scale hunting expeditions; the victims, even the ants, are always used for food. The corpses of their own adult dead, however, are usually spared; these serve as food only in case of extreme need. The expeditions of the so-called hunting or driver ants are organized somewhat differently. We have numerous descriptions of the campaigns of the South American *Eciton* species, most of which are blind, and of the African *Anomma* species (cf. Fig. 17). Vosseler gives an excellent account of the Ethiopian hunting ant which the Africans call *siafu:*

"The nomadic ants are imbued with a restless spirit. Wherever they go, you see nothing but hustling, hunting, battle, and murder. First a few scouts appear, rushing restlessly back and forth, sounding out the terrain. Before one is aware of their purpose, impatient hordes begin to pour out of a little cleft in the earth; the hole soon widens, and as if by magic hundreds turn to thousands and hundreds of thousands. Like a shoreless river they pour in all directions over the ground and the low shrubbery, covering the earth with their dense swarm. A mad scampering begins on all sides. Crickets, cockroaches, spiders, caterpillars, maggots—any creatures

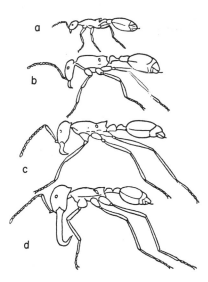

FIG. 17 *a-d.* Legionary or driver ants (*Eciton hamatum*). (After Wheeler.) *a*) Worker. *b*) Intermediate form. *c*) Soldier. *d*) Large soldier with greatly enlarged jaws.

large or small, armed or unarmed, that may have felt secure in their cover—take aimless and headlong flight from the ruthless army.

"Now begins a silent, bloody drama with scarcely its equal for excitement. A great bear-caterpillar loses its confidence in the protective covering of its long hairs and races with bent back along the edge of the path, followed by the ants as by a pack of bloodthirsty wild dogs. The chase continues up a steep wall, the hunters on the heels of the game. The caterpillar slips down, and for a moment the ants lose the trail. But before the game can get to its feet again, twenty ants have bitten fast into its hair; in an instant it is covered by hundreds of them, cut to pieces, and immediately dragged nestward by the hunters, who are heedless of the difficulties of the terrain. A cricket summons up all the strength of its sinewy legs to spring out of danger—in vain. It is surrounded, held fast by its legs, feelers, and wings, and skillfully dissected by dozens of sharp jaws; the pieces follow those of the caterpillar.

"The field is quickly swept clean by the forward swarming ants. Now the reserves march up six to ten abreast, forming columns one or two fingers wide, which relieve or reinforce the troops at the front. Where the murderous swarm has passed roads are taking shape, weaving in and out in a dense network. Along these roads fresh soldiers advance while others haul the booty to the rear. The embattled confusion moves forward. The highways are smoothed out, and their sides are occupied by sentries. These large soldiers stand 'shoulder to shoulder' at right angles to the road, their heads in constant movement as they watch for intruders.

"At the slightest sign of a foe the sentries rear up, thorax and head erect, and rest their antennae on their wide-open pincers, poised to attack. If no enemy shows up, the sentries are reduced in number; the giants and a few others line the roads at irregular intervals, head upraised, feelers tingling, jaws in readiness. Their flanks secured, the diligent ants stream along for days. Often there is a two-way traffic, one army advancing while another, heavily laden, makes its way back to the nest. But these nomadic ants never inhabit a nest for long; like gypsies, they have no permanent home and soon move on with bag and baggage, hunting and waging war as they go." I myself have seen similar expeditions in the jungle of the upper Paraná.

The scene is very much the same when these ant armies

swarm over a human dwelling. Everybody leaves—insects, animals, and men. Since the ants quickly move on, the house is soon habitable again, and a visit from the ant hordes is not always unwelcome; for all the vermin, including rats, mice, and even snakes, are destroyed or driven away.

These warlike ants are sometimes a boon to other organisms. In the *Cecropia* trees of Brazil there lives a little black ant, the *Azteca*. It is extremely fierce and keeps a good many insects away from the tree. For a long time certain characteristics of the *Cecropia* were regarded as adaptations by which the tree "enticed" the *Azteca* to make its home in it. The leaves of the *Cecropia* bear certain bulbous growths which the ants eat, and the trunk is composed of thin-walled cavities which the ants can easily pierce and use as dwellings. The same was said of many tropical acacias which have edible bulbs on their leaves and bear hollow thorns in which ants can lodge. Recent observations, however, lead us to doubt that these facts follow any natural law. Although the plants are sometimes protected by their pugnacious inhabitants, the one can occur without the other. The *Cecropia* tree in particular does perfectly well without ants. "The *Cecropia* tree needs the *Azteca* ants no more than a dog needs fleas," said von Ihering, who has made the closest study of these colonies. The ants can also live elsewhere, although the tree will provide them with shelter and a part of their food.

Another plant that is famous as an ant-dwelling is the *Myrmecodia* (Fig. 18), which grows on trees in the Malay Archipelago. It is a kind of tuber full of hollow spaces, which presumably serve as water reservoirs. These caverns, which provide an ideal dwelling for ants, are of two sorts: one has smooth, light-brown walls, while the walls of the other are blackish and are covered with little bumps. In the first kind the ants deposit

their larvae and cocoons; the bumpy chambers serve as
a kind of toilet in which the ants put their excrement. On
the dung grows a smoky-gray fungus which accounts for
the blackness of the cell walls. The ants keep this lawn
of fungus short by nibbling at it, but it probably does
not serve them as food; more likely, it is a kind of weed.

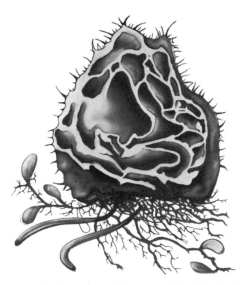

FIG. 18. Ant plant (*Myrmecodia*). The hollow spaces serve the
ants as dwellings.

It was formerly believed that insects and plants of
this sort went hand in hand; for example, these hollow
bulbs were thought to owe their existence to the ants.
It turns out, however, that although *Myrmecodia* bene-
fits from the ant manure it grows in the same way without the ants. As with *Cecropia*, the ants profit most; in
Myrmecodia they find protection and moisture and in
Cecropia shelter and food. These, of course, are their
primary needs, as the next section will show in greater
detail.

Food and Shelter

The whole ant colony revolves around the offspring, and the food and lodging of the coming generation are of great concern. The thousands of species of ants feed and shelter their broods in many different ways. To describe them all would take up many pages, and in almost every case I should be obliged to add subspecies and exceptions, often extending down to the individual ant. Instead, let us take a look at some of the best-known ants in their native environment to see how they master the problems of food and lodging.

Wherever ants settle, certain fundamental conditions must be met. The basic foods, fats, carbohydrates, and proteins (which humans also require), must be within reach. It may seem that such a variety of things would be hard to get, but the mother who sends her child to school with a salami sandwich has solved the problem without knowing it existed. We get fats and proteins in butter, milk, and meat. Carbohydrates and proteins come from various vegetables and from baked goods, the starch of which is transformed into sugars by our digestive juices; we also get sugar directly from fruits. Ants usually get all of their sugar directly, although some are capable of transforming starch into sugar. For fats and proteins they depend chiefly on meat —including insects, spiders, small animals, and in the case of hunting ants, larger game.

Ants require shelter and an amount of warmth and humidity that varies with the species. Ants that live in cool damp regions require additional heat and must take measures against excessive dampness; in hot dry countries the exact opposite is the case. As a result, the way ants feed and house themselves varies greatly over the world. Let us examine a few such cases.

Wood Ants

The whole of Central Europe would be a damp cool forest land if it had not been cultivated by man. The wood ant (*Formica rufa*), with which our discussion began, is characteristic of this region. Let us take a look at his dwelling. The wood ant shows a distinct preference for evergreen forests, building its familiar mounds chiefly of pine needles and small branches. Beneath the mound the nest reaches far into the earth, and in the winter one must dig deep to find the ants. The purpose of the mound is to catch as much as possible of the sun's warmth, particularly in the cool spring and autumn. A lodging burrowed into the earth provides little surface for the rays of the sun to fall on, but the mound catches the slanting rays of the morning and evening sun. At these times the brood is brought up into the mound; in the noonday heat, it is carried below (Fig. 19). Another advantage of the loosely built mound is that it drains quickly after heavy rains; the workers are always busy enlarging the hill and adding new material.

The nest must constantly be supplied with food. Everything that the region offers is used: small insects that the workers can kill in single combat as well as the larger creatures that require a mass attack by poison and are carried back in pieces. Actual counts show that each day a nest of wood ants destroys several thousands of caterpillars, butterflies, flies, beetles, and other small insects, most of which are harmful to man. This useful police-

FIG. 19. Mound and nest of the wood ant (*Formica rufa*).
The pine needles and other material, collected from far
about, are piled up over the main part of the nest to catch
the heat of the sun (cf. Fig. 20).

man of the forest is now rigorously protected by law and
is even artificially introduced into some regions.

The colony usually includes a number of mounds
connected by paths. Observations have shown that the
wood ant's hunting ground may extend for hundreds of
yards, and a sketch of the central nests and dependent
colonies looks exactly like a map of a human settlement.
Paths fan out on all sides, sometimes leading up into the
treetops. The ants climb the trees in search of sugar,
which they get from plant lice or aphids. We shall say
more about this later on.

Another wood ant that develops an intricate system
of pathways—and also keeps plant lice—is the jet-black
Lasius fuliginosus. It makes its home in tree trunks or
under roots in open deciduous forests. This ant digs

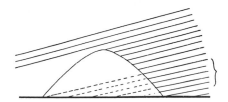

FIG. 20. The mounds of the wood ant store up the heat of the sun. When the sun is low in the sky the part inhabited by the ants receives warmth only from the rays indicated by dotted lines; the domelike structure makes many more rays available for warming the nest.

passages in rotten wood, mixing the chewed-up wood with sticky spittle to produce a kind of crude cardboard; from this material it builds what looks like a wasp's nest. In the tropics such cardboard nests are often found hanging in the open.

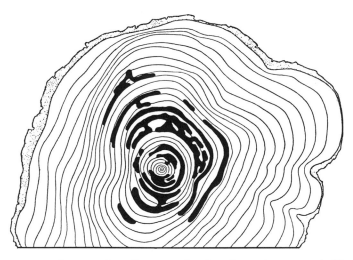

FIG. 21. Cross section of a tree, showing the nest passages built by the carpenter ant (*Camponotus herculaneus*).

FIG. 22. Tree nest of *Colobopsis truncata.*
The soldiers are distinguished by thick heads
with which they can "cork up" the entrances
to the nest.

Cardboard nests are also built in our latitudes by the
carpenter ants of the genus *Camponotus* (Fig. 4). With
their sharp and powerful jaws the *Camponotus* can gnaw
their way into sound wood, and they often do considerable harm when they make their nests in the beams of
houses (Fig. 21). In spite of their size they are very
timid and as a rule come out only at dusk or at night,
when they sally forth like the wood ant on pillaging
expeditions or to visit the aphids.

The *Colobopsis* species, which are closely related to
the carpenter ants, are fully adapted to living in the
trees. In Central Europe they build their passages chiefly
in the upper branches of nut trees. The soldiers, with their
thick, flattened heads, are admirably equipped for block-
ing the narrow passages gnawed in the wood. Fig. 22
shows a soldier corking up the entrance to a nest; the

"cork" is made particularly effective by the fact that the flattened head looks like tree bark.

Camponotus senex, which lives in the trees of tropical jungles, makes a nest out of bundles of leaves tied together with threads. These spun nests, which are also made by the genus *Oecophylla* in the woods of southern Asia and the Sunda Islands, were at first a source of mystification, for the ants have no spinning glands. Was it possible that the ants used the only spinners in the colony, their larvae, to do the weaving? This notion, which was first rejected as fantastic, proved correct. *Oecophylla,*

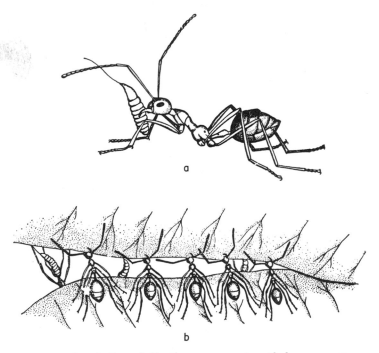

FIG. 23 *a-b. a*) *Oecophylla,* the weaver ant, with larva secreting a thread. *b*) Weaver ants holding leaves together; behind the leaves are two other ants with larvae. (After Wheeler.)

FIG. 24. Nest of the weaver ant (*Oe-cophylla*), consisting of leaves woven together with the threads spun by larvae.

the weaver ant, actually uses its larvae as distaff and shuttle (Fig. 23 *a*). When leaves are to be woven into a nest, a number of workers first march up to pull the edges of the leaves together. They grip the edge of one leaf with their jaws and hook their legs into the other (Fig. 23 *b*). Sometimes, when there is a wide space between the leaves, the workers form chains, grasping one another about the waist with their jaws.

As soon as the leaves are brought together, other workers come from the nest. Each of these workers carries a larva between its jaws (Fig. 23 *a* left), squeezing it a little to stimulate the activity of the big spinning gland. The worker presses the larva's head (where the gland duct is situated) to the edge of one leaf, then moves it across to the other leaf. This operation is repeated over and over, until finally a strong mesh of crisscrossing threads is formed between the leaves.

The use by these ants of a tool not provided by their own bodies sets them off as a rarity in the animal kingdom. Tools were long thought to be an exclusive characteristic of man. Although this is untrue (the apes, for example, use stones for cracking nuts), the use of tools is most uncommon even among the higher vertebrates. Its "implement" enables the weaver ant to live in trees and to build solid nests, without—like related varieties —digging passageways in the wood, a labor for which it is not equipped.

People have, in turn, found a special use for these ants' nests. The relatively large *Oecophylla* ants, which measure from ¼ to ⅖ inch in length, are extremely warlike, and no other insects can survive in the trees they inhabit. The dangling nests (Fig. 24) are easily cut down. The Chinese wrap the nests in gauze or similar material, cut them down, and then hang them on other trees that they wish to protect against insects—chiefly the Chinese citrus trees, which are subject to attack by aphids and other pests. The weaver ants check these parasites, and in some localities the trade in *Oecophylla* nests has assumed considerable proportions.

Meadow Ants

The meadow ants which we find in our gardens and fields are adapted to an entirely different environment from that of the wood ants. They require no trees and for the most part stay on the ground. First among these we may mention the garden ant (*Lasius niger*). The hills built by the meadow ant are entirely different from those of the wood ant: they consist of earth thrown out of the nest, which often lies deep underground. The earth is piled up amid stalks of grass and other plants, which help to support it, and serves as an extension of the ant's dwelling (Fig. 25). As a rule the hill lasts only a short time; a heavy rainfall or a spell of drought and the structure collapses. Consequently, such hills are usually seen in the spring, when, like the mounds of other ants, they serve to catch the oblique rays of the sun.

More solidly built are the mounds of the yellow *Lasius,* which in general prefers wet regions and may even settle in swampy meadows and bogs. In such regions these ants are constantly imperiled by excessive moisture and by the encroachment of peat mosses, which flourish in the soil the ants have loosened. That they nevertheless survive is shown by the numerous mounds which sometimes give a whole landscape its characteristic imprint, as in certain parts of the Iser Mountains in Silesia.

This geological activity on the part of the ants, with the characteristic landscapes it produces, is none too frequent in our latitudes, but in other regions it is important enough to have attracted much attention in re-

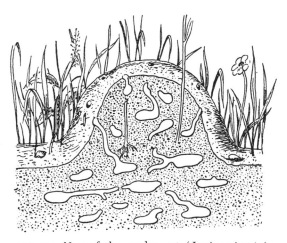

FIG. 25. Nest of the garden ant (*Lasius niger*) in a meadow; below, the passages extending deep into the ground; above, the mound of earth thrown up from the nest, surrounded by blades of grass. The mound is also traversed by passages.

cent years. The ants dig deep into the ground and bring up soil from strata far beneath the surface. In certain steppes they unearth rich red clay, which gradually forms a layer of fertile humus covering the light barren sand. The stones under which the ants have made their tunnels gradually sink into the earth. A particularly impressive geological movement of this sort has been observed in Australia: many slopes have been eroded as the rains wash away the soft earth brought up from below by the ants.

A similar movement of the earth's strata can be observed on a small scale in our latitudes, in our gardens, playgrounds, and roads. It is usually harmful. Where man has spread a layer of topsoil or sand on the surface of the ground, the ants may undo his work by bringing up a layer of subsoil. The chief offenders are garden ants or little pavement ants (*Myrmica* and *Tetramorium*), which live in hiding and attract notice only by this kind of activity. We find them in large numbers under stones; the stones accumulate warmth, which encourages the ants to bring up their broods.

The last of the meadow ants we shall talk about lives his whole life underground. This is the thieving *Solenopsis fugax*. These tiny creatures, often only $\frac{6}{100}$ inch long, like to build their edifices in the vicinity of other ants. They dig passages just big enough to crawl through. Through these tunnels they attack the nests of larger ants. Instead of hunting on their own account, they eat the provisions and even the brood of the other ants. Once they have completed their meal they withdraw into their own narrow galleries, which are too small to admit their victims.

Desert Ants

The tropical and subtropical species of *Solenopsis* that venture into the desert have a hard time finding sustenance. In the desert they face the special problems of all desert ants. The main difficulty is to find water and moisture. Warmth is no problem; on the contrary, the desert ants must protect themselves and their brood against excessive heat. For this purpose, they dig passages many yards deep, until they reach the ground water. The earth removed from the passages is piled up about the entrance in the form of a small crater, like the mouth of a volcano (Fig. 26). The hills of such crater nests, as they are called, are not at all like the mounds of the wood ant; they are not deliberately constructed but are simple piles of refuse. To these piles of dirt the ants often add other refuse, remnants of food or the corpses of members of the colony—a phenomenon we have witnessed on a small scale among certain of the meadow ants. Sometimes the rubbish is neatly separated: to one side the remnants of devoured insects, to the other the corpses of the colony's own dead (Fig. 27). These piles of corpses are the so-called ant cemeteries. Crater nests may be observed under excellent conditions in the shiny black and red ant of the Chilean Atacama Desert region. This species (*Dorymyrmex goetschi*) was named after me by a colleague because I "discovered" it—that is, first brought it to Europe for description.

The nests usually have only a few entrances, which

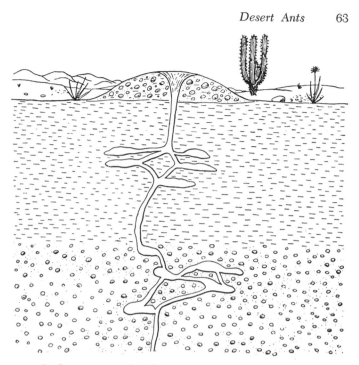

FIG. 26. Crater nests of a desert ant (*Pogonomyrmex*). The passages penetrate deep into the soil and connect with chambers to the right and left. The earth thrown up from the different strata forms a crater-like elevation in which there are no passages (cf. Fig. 34).

may be far apart; around these entrances the excavated material is piled into craters. The Atacama Desert is rich in mineral deposits; veins of copper, silver, and gold occur close to the surface, becoming more abundant deeper down. Grains of sand that contain gold will sometimes be found in the ant craters, or we may see an ant hauling little grains of dark green copper ore (Fig. 28). In such cases the ants have burrowed down into ore deposits that are not visible from the surface.

In the Preface I mentioned Herodotus' reference to gold-mining ants. Here we have confirmation of his as-

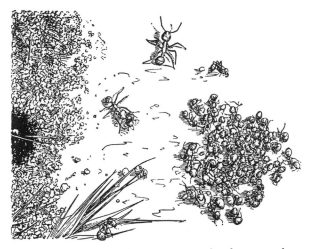

FIG. 27. Ant cemetery. The corpses of colony members are not eaten, but are thrown out of the nest and sometimes piled up in a heap like other useless objects. (Drawn from a photograph.)

sertion, which was long regarded as pure fantasy. Of course, the insect does not "know" what it is carrying; as far as the ant is concerned, the gold or copper ore is nothing but earth that must be removed from its dwelling. But this activity can be helpful to man. According to a recent newspaper story, miners in the mountains of New Mexico use the ant craters to plot the course of veins containing manganese.

The depth of these ore deposits is not easy to determine. It may amount to several yards. Although we know that the passages are sometimes this long, it has not been possible to dig them up. Sometimes the material in which the ants build is too hard, sometimes it is too dry and dusty, and in the latter case the whole edifice collapses as one digs. For this reason, I made several attempts to explore the ants' passages with the help of an "Ariadne's thread." I caught an ant, attached a fine silk thread to it, and let it loose. The ant hurried for the nest and crawled as deep as it could to escape the enemy. By measuring the thread I was able to determine the length of the passage—at least to tell how far the ant ran. One cannot, of course, claim great accuracy for this method.

The Atacama ant has a hard time getting food. It runs swiftly about, constantly searching for nourishment. Among the bare stones of the desert one can observe these searching forays from a considerable distance; observation would be next to impossible if the terrain were less open, for the ants dash along singly in zigzags or spirals and almost never go in a straight line (Fig. 47). They explore considerable areas, and I often found ants as much as 75 feet from their nest. This method of search, which has also been observed among other desert ants, is made necessary by the rarity of the food supply. The items that my ants hauled home were the dried up or rotting remains of insects or other small animals that had somehow been blown into the desert.

Another long-legged, swift-moving desert ant, originally from Asia, now abounds in Capri and other Mediterranean islands. It seems to have arrived not very long ago and found favorable conditions. This ant, *Acantholepis frauenfeldi,* is distinguished by a highly expandable

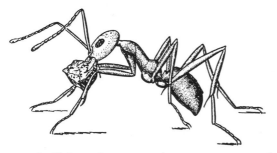

FIG. 28. Chilean desert ant (*Dorymyrmex goetschi*). This ant builds crater nests (cf. Fig. 26) and sometimes burrows down to deep ore deposits in which it builds its chambers. The ant in the figure is carrying a crumb of copper ore.

abdomen, a gift of the first importance for desert ants. Whenever they find one of the rare sources of liquid food, they pump themselves full and carry a large quantity home for distribution among their companions (cf. Fig. 42).

The distensible crop and abdomen of *Acantholepis frauenfeldi* bring to mind the so-called honeypots or honey carriers among the desert ants. The name honeypots was first coined for certain *Myrmecocystus* ants living in southern Colorado. Among the workers of these species we find a remarkable variant, workers with immense abdomens distended almost to the bursting point. The community develops these honeypots artificially; choosing newborn workers with very elastic skin, the other workers stuff them with honey. The crop is packed so full that it occupies the entire abdomen; this leaves

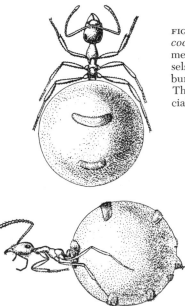

FIG. 29. Honeypots of *Myrmecocystus*. A few of the colony members, used as storage vessels, are filled almost to the bursting point with sweet juices. They are then hung in special chambers.

so little room for other organs such as the midgut that they were first believed to be absent (cf. Fig. 29).

These honeypots or honey carriers are nothing but living storehouses. Since the *Myrmecocystus* lives almost exclusively on the juice of certain galls growing on scrub oaks, the ant has every reason to lay up provisions. The galls exude their sweet juice only during the short period when the larva of the gall wasp, which provokes their growth, is developing inside them. If the ants wish to avoid a shortage of the sweet juices during the lean months, they must store them in one way or another. Unable to secrete wax and build cells like the bees, they have found their own answer in the honeypots. The colony sallies forth in long files in search of the gall honey. On their return they pump the honeypots full. Obviously, such inflated creatures cannot take part in the work of the colony; in fact they can scarcely move. They spend the greater part of their lives hanging motionless in chambers whose ceilings are especially constructed for them to hang from. The yellowish honey in their abdomens makes them look like little Japanese lanterns (Fig. 30).

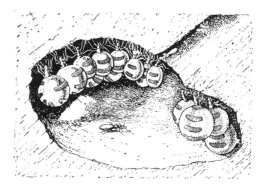

FIG. 30. Hanging honeypots of the desert ant *Myrmecocystus*. (After Wheeler.)

I discovered a less extreme form of honeypot at the edge of the Atacama Desert in Chile, a region characterized by giant cactuses. Here lives an inconspicuous little desert ant (*Tapinoma antarcticum*), which usually attracts notice only when it moves from its nest in search of more favorable territory. Now and then honey carriers that have not become entirely immobile can be seen hobbling along in such processions (Fig. 31). The carriers are not always filled with honey; they sometimes carry the juice of the giant cactus, which the normal workers draw from the base of the cactus stems.

These ants make shallow nests at the edge of the desert, under stones and similar objects, and do not need to sink passages deep into the earth, as do the crater builders who find their moisture underground. I have also seen them bringing in grass seeds, which will provide both food and moisture in times of shortage.

FIG. 31. A worker and a water carrier of the Chilean desert ant *Tapinoma antarcticum*. These water carriers are not so disfigured as are the honeypots in Figs. 29 and 30.

Outside the desert zone proper, in the dry bushy steppe, the *Tapinoma* ants undergo a slight change; they become smaller, and there are no longer extreme honeypots and water carriers among them. Within one species we find all sorts of gradations from normal workers to highly modified forms. These may be regarded as intermediate links in the series leading from *Acantholepis* (Fig. 42), in which the entire colony is equipped with greatly distensible abdomens, to the genuine and extreme honey-pots of the *Myrmecocystus* (Fig. 29).

Some desert ants obtain their food supply in another way—by collecting grains and seeds. But since this takes us to a different group with entirely different habits, we shall treat it in a special section.

Granaries and Fungus Gardens

Ant granaries have been known since the most ancient times. Perhaps for this very reason our accounts of such phenomena were so intermingled with myths and fairy tales that we were very late in arriving at a true interpretation of them. In his Proverbs, King Solomon used as an example the ants that bring in grain to fill their storehouses. As the collecting of seeds cannot be observed in Northern Europe, modern students of ants first thought that the ancients had made a mistake, that the objects transported were not grains but ant pupae. But then in Italy, southern Spain, Dalmatia, Hungary, Greece, and Provence, observers came across the harvester ants of the genus *Messor*, which move in long files transporting seeds. Exploration of these nests, which usually take the form of craters, led to the discovery of the granaries themselves.

What happens to the stored-up grains long remained a mystery. It had been noted that the ants carry the grains rather haphazardly into the upper galleries of the nest and that the supplies often include snail shells and other such objects. In the upper part of the nest the grains are sorted and "threshed"—that is, the husk is stripped off (Figs. 32 and 33). The seeds thus processed are stored in granaries situated a little deeper down.

Since the grains almost never germinate in the granaries, it was supposed that the ants had some means of preventing germination. Another hypothesis proposed that the ants actually provoked germination, for they

FIGS. 32 and 33. Harvester ants (*Messor*) husking seeds.

were often observed carrying sprouted seeds in from the area around the nest. The piles of bitten-off seedlings found around the nest were interpreted as an indication that the ants purposely provoked a malting process, as brewers do, in order to turn the starch in the seeds into sugar.

Still another explanation was offered. Observers claimed that a part of the husked and sprouted grain was worked into a doughlike mass which was baked in the sun along with the dry seeds. The baking was thought to "sterilize" the ant bread, so that only a certain variety of fungus "desired" by the ants could grow, and so on. Other investigators worked out less complicated systems, but all of them had to rely on guesswork, for no one had ever seen ants eating grains.

When my attention was called to the strange behavior of these ants I resolved to get to the bottom of it. It soon became clear that specialized observation would

FIG. 34. Frame nest for the observation of ants' building activities. Harvester ants are installed in a glass-covered frame measuring 14 inches square. A glass tube (T) serves to moisten the earth from below. A_1-A_2 designates the original surface of the ground before the ants dug their shafts. Waste piles are situated at A_1 and A_2. Such an artificial nest represents a cross section of a crater nest (cf. Fig. 26).

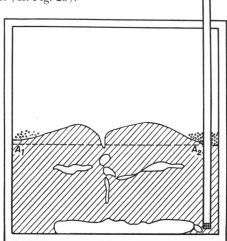

not suffice and that a thorough study of the biology and psychology of the ants would be necessary—for a seemingly irrelevant fact will often clear up mysteries of this sort.

It was the harvesters' building operations that provided the key. To study these operations I enclosed *Messor* colonies in upright plaster frames with glass walls on both sides, so that the earth of the nests could be moistened both from above and from the side (Fig. 34). It turned out that the moistened earth releases the building urge in ants that are not occupied. When the earth was moistened the ants went to work fanatically, even throwing out any grains that were mixed with the earth. The contagion spread to all unemployed individuals in the vicinity. No division of labor according to size could be observed; the large soldiers worked just as ardently as did the smaller workers. The soldiers carried out an average of one crumb of earth every two minutes; this activity continued for hours. If we spread grain about the entrance, the workers would eagerly set about carrying it in. When the inhabitants of a nest were in this fashion induced to build and to gather grains at the same time, the two teams took no heed of one another. Both worked with equal zeal; sometimes the same seeds were brought in by one team and carried out again by the other.

As building was carried on only when the soil was moist, and seeds were collected when it was dry, some investigators came to the false conclusion that the ants carried the seeds into the moisture to make them sprout, thus starting a malting process that would be slowed down or stopped when the ground dried. Further experiments, however, showed that this complicated treatment of the grain was quite unnecessary. The ants use both sprouted and unsprouted seeds, as long as they can be opened. If one helps the ants by crushing the grain or boring a hole in the husk, they use the whole supply. Where both crushed and sprouted seeds are available, the ants prefer the former. The only advantage of germination is that the hole made by the sprout gives the ants access to the inside of the seed.

Next, as a rule, the so-called, "chewing societies" get to work. A number of ants assemble and chew for hours on the contents of the seeds (Fig. 35). In this way they produce ant bread, which is eaten immediately or, if there is too much of it, carried to the storerooms. In their communal chewing, to which meat may also be subjected, the ants secrete large quantities of saliva; the chewing and salivation transform starch into sugar, as may be proved by chemical tests. With its abundance of

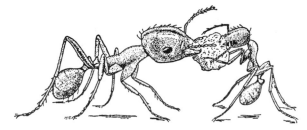

FIG. 35. Worker and soldier of harvester ants (*Messor*) chewing together at the content of a seed ("chewing society" for the production of "ant bread").

sugar the ant bread is an excellent food for both adult ants and their brood. Sugar thus produced may also be transformed into liquid and stored in the crops of the chewers; although this has not been proved, direct observation shows that the more the ant bread is chewed the softer it becomes, and that it vanishes almost entirely.

The harvesters' manner of using their seeds is much simpler than had been thought, and the answer to the question of why earlier observers never saw the *Messor* ants eating grains is just as simple: the ants in the artificial nests were too well treated—above all, too well fed. If one gives sugar, honey, and so on, to these ants, they have no need to open the seeds they have collected; they continue to bring them home, but take no further interest in them. The same is true under natural conditions: the granaries serve only to provide supplies for the cold rainy season or the hot summer, when it becomes difficult or impossible for the ants to obtain other food—which in the *Messor* species includes insects.

Harvester ants of the genus *Pogonomyrmex* live in South and Central America, and as far north as Texas. They too have given rise to a legend. Since grasses of the kinds most favored by the ants are sometimes found growing luxuriantly around the crater openings, it was believed that they planted their grain in order to provide themselves with a nearby source of seeds. This agricultural skill also proved to be a fable. The grasses sprout from seeds that the ants have lost in the vicinity of the nest or carried out while they were building; if the seeds fall in good soil it is purely by accident.

The granaries of the harvester ants help us to understand the special habits of the fungus growers, which occupy one of the highest ranks in ant civilization. We have seen that the *Messor* species often work their grains into the crumbly mass known as ant bread, which is sometimes not eaten at once but stored away. Fungi may grow on this bread and in some instances it is not the crumbs but the fungi that are eaten. Other ants bring home vegetable matter that cannot be eaten but serves to fertilize the crumbly mass in which the fungi grow. The *Messor* ants, with their mania for collecting things, will drag bits of leaves or stems into the nest if they find no suitable

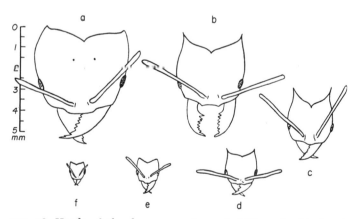

FIG. 36. Heads of the fungus-growing ant (*Atta columbica*). *a*) Large soldier (giant) with a trace of the frontal eyes, characteristic of the queens, which are absent in the other workers and soldiers (cf. also Fig. 10). *b*) Soldier. *c-e*) Small soldiers, transitional forms, workers. *f*) Minims.

seeds, but they have not yet reached the point of true fungus culture; nor have the Spanish *Aphaenogasters,* which I have occasionally seen cutting leaves and bringing them home. These cases, however, bring us to the true fungus growers. Certain ants of South and Central America—and only in these regions—have taken the final step. They chew up the collected leaves to produce a kind of compost heap in which the mycelia or fungus filaments develop. It is these ants that cultivate fungus "gardens."

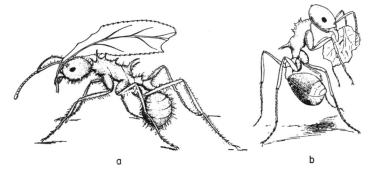

a   b

FIG. 37 *a-b.* *a*) Leaf-cutting ant (*Acromyrmex*) carrying home a fragment of a leaf. *b*) The fragment is chewed up in the nest.

The operations of these ants have been the subject of frequent studies, for in the tropical regions of South and Central America their activities cause considerable damage and have attracted a good deal of attention to the ants. The various species of *Atta* and *Acromyrmex* are relatively large ants, including all the gradations from minims to giants (Fig. 36). They always march out in long files, sometimes by day but more often by night, making their way to a tree or bush. With their sharp mandibles they cut pieces out of the leaves, and for this reason they have been called leafcutters. While new hordes march up, the first move back to the nest in a long chain, each ant holding a piece of leaf over its head like an umbrella (Fig. 37 *a*). The Latin Americans call them porters. Observers racked their brains wondering what the ants, which are ordinarily accustomed to better fare, did with these inedible leaves. The correct solution, at first dimly suspected, was finally established by a close investigation.

The leafcutters do not feed on the leaves themselves. Once the leaf particles are brought into the nest, they are chewed up like the seeds of the harvesters (Fig. 37 *b*). The resultant spongelike mass, full of passages and hollows, is the so-called fungus garden, which is always

FIG. 38. Fungus gardens of the leafcutter ants (*Atta*).

situated in a special chamber far under the ground. Here grow the fungus strands or mycelia (Fig. 38). When the ants bite off the mycelia, little heads—called kohlrabi or, more poetically, ambrosia—are formed. These little heads and the bunches of fungus strands contain important vitamins and sources of energy; they are the favorite food of the American *Atta* and *Acromyrmex* species, particularly for their broods. Until recently, the fungi raised by the ants were thought to be members of the genus *Rhozites,* which occurs nowhere else. This is not the case. The genus *Hypomyces,* which is found in the fungus gardens, also grows semiparasitically on the boletus. Fungus gardens of *Hypomyces* fungi artificially cultivated in Breslau, Germany, were placed in artificial ants' nests; the South American leafcutters that lived in the nests took the fungus gardens and continued to cultivate them.

People once thought that, like human gardeners, special gardener ants had to weed the undesirable fungi out of the compost heaps. This myth has since been exploded. The "cultivated" strain thrives on the chewed leaves mixed with spittle; the harmful mold fungi, with certain exceptions, do not. Unless this mixture of chewed-up leaves and saliva is placed in the beds, harmful fungus strands may quickly spread, rendering the beds useless.

The Brazilian *Atta* and the Argentine *Acromyrmex* ants spread their fungus from colony to colony, storing it from generation to generation. The queen preparing for the marriage flight always takes with her bits of the fungus from her native nest, carrying them in a little pocket under her mouth. After she has been fertilized in the marriage flight and has sealed herself up in the ground, her first care is for the fungus. She vomits it up and immediately manures it with her own excrement, which is the only fertilizer she has available. Tearing off a bit of the fungus, she holds it close to the tip of her abdomen and lets a drop of excrement drip over it. Then she sets it down and treats the other bits in the same way. After a time a fungus garden springs up (Fig. 40). But even a queen ant cannot change the laws of metabolism. If she is to manure her fungus garden, she must have food. Like other young queens we have observed, she eats her own eggs—90 per cent of them or more—in order to

FIG. 39. Cultivated fungus with kohlrabi heads, the food of the leaf-cutter ants (*Atta*).

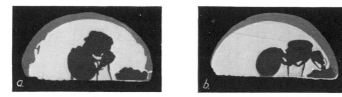

FIG. 40 *a-b*. Young queen of the leafcutter ant (*Atta sexdens*) laying out the fungus garden. *a*) The young queen holds a bit of fungus to her hindgut to fertilize it. *b*) The fertilized bit of fungus is put in the garden. These photographs by J. Huber are among the first made of ants. They are reproduced partly for their historical interest.

nourish herself and produce sufficient manure for her fungus.

The first minims the queen raises feed on eggs at the start, but they also come to their mother's help at once and begin to manure the garden on their own. Once the first little heads of kohlrabi appear, the famine is ended; then, after eight to ten days, the workers dig a passage into the open and begin to cut their own leaves. The garden grows and furnishes its vegetables and the queen can now permit all her eggs to develop. The new workers that are being born extend the nest in all directions and start their assault on the greenery—providing the biologist with an absorbing study, but doing no end of harm to the trees.

The most interesting thing about the leafcutter ants, in addition to their highly developed social life, is this: they use a raw material, available in large quantities but of little food value, to make another substance that meets their nutritive needs. Their colonies need only harvest leaves, always abundant in the jungle, to be totally independent of the risks of hunting expeditions. They have no need of meat or other high-quality food. By transforming a worthless substance into a useful one they have achieved a degree of self-sufficiency that many human economic planners would envy.

The *Atta* ants stand at the summit of ant civilization not only in their economic life but also in their military prowess and fecundity. Every member of the colony is well armored, being so heavily covered with prickles that he is extremely unpleasant to touch (Figs. 36 and 37). The soldiers, which are of different sizes, possess effective weapons in their powerful jaws (Fig. 36). They can inflict bloody wounds even on humans. In population the *Atta* nests outdo all others. Even among ants their queen is remarkable for her fecundity. In a single year, as we have mentioned, an *Atta* queen has been known to produce 3,500 winged females and 35,000 males—nearly 40,000 sexually developed offspring, which represent only a small percentage of her total progeny. The population of an *Atta* colony must be estimated at several millions.

When large numbers of these gigantic colonies attack coffee or maté plantations they will obviously do a great deal of harm. The high degree of organization which biologists so much admire in their colonies has nevertheless earned them the title of Public Enemy Number One among the coffee growers of southern Brazil. A merciless war has been declared on them, but so far little progress has been made in curtailing the plague.

Aphid Tenders and Honey Ants

Next to the harvesters and fungus growers, the ants with the highest degree of social organization are those that derive their food from aphids, or plant lice. Here, too, we find different degrees of adaptation, and again we must distinguish between truth and poetry. At the final stage of development there is no doubt that ants and aphids are wholly adapted to one another. Some of our garden ants are known to have close ties with plant lice. But the widespread belief that our garden ants drive the plant lice out to pasture like cows or carry them to their grazing grounds in trees or bushes is unfounded.

The great assemblies of plant lice that led people to this idea can form even when there are no ants around. The eggs of the plant lice lie dormant during the winter; in the spring they produce females which, without fertilization, bear numerous offspring. One such mother was observed to bear upwards of 20 young in one day; the lice are born fully developed and ready to join their elders. Under favorable conditions we may see 80 to 100 plant lice gathered together where only a short time before there was but a single female. All are busily occupied sucking the juices of plants. They suck more than they need, and the ants, as we shall see, benefit by the surplus.

This is how the ants find their cows. A scout runs across a gathering of plant lice, returns home, and alerts the colony. The ants pour out toward the new feeding ground along the track already laid by the scout. If we paint a ring of glue around the branch where the lice are

FIG. 41. Garden ant (*Lasius niger*) with aphids.

assembled, not a single ant will reach them, but the colony of lice will be there just the same. "But you sometimes see ants carrying plant lice," an attentive observer might argue. And he would be right. If he had looked closely, however, he would have seen, in the case of garden ants, wood ants, and carpenter ants, that the aphids are not carried up the branch toward the assembly point but down the ants' nest. Furthermore, he would observe that the louse is usually dead or dying. These ants use the lice not only as milk cows but also as a source of meat.

This observation brings us one step closer to an understanding of how the relation between ant and aphid must have developed. The ants, as we have already seen, are almost without exception omniverous; in short, they require meat and sugar. Almost all the meat they need is provided by insects; they either drag dead insects into their nest or attack and overpower live ones. When their prey is not sufficient, there is always a reserve: they do not hesitate to fall back on their own brood, even the queen joining in. The need for sugar is often harder to satisfy. The harvester ants transform the starchy content of seeds into sugar; others consume the highly diluted sugar solutions offered by certain plants.

In the spring we see ants, like the bees, visiting flowers and carrying home the nectar. They may also draw the sweet sap from the so-called extrafloral nectaries, those strange cuplike organs on the leaf stems of passion flowers and other plants. In their search for honey they may come upon various insects that secrete sweet substances —some leafhoppers, shield lice, and plant lice. Here they find sugar in a highly concentrated solution, for these insects possess long sucking tubes, often longer than the rest of the body, with which they drill into the various parts of plants and suck out the juices so efficiently that they cannot use the whole supply. The insects utilize only a small part of the nectar they consume; the rest, in concentrated form, is exuded in a clear, sweet drop from the tip of the abdomen. If no ants are present to lick it up, this juice flows over the leaves or is squirted out, so that it sometimes literally rains down from the trees. This is "manna from heaven" for the ants, and often we see them licking it up at a distance from the aphid colony. When they meet an aphid, they lick up

its honey; if there is none, they act as they do when begging a fellow ant for food: they tickle the louse with
their feelers until the drop is produced.

The aphid produces honey from its hindgut. The thin
little tubes found in certain aphids, which some observers
still regard as udders, secrete instead of honey an unpleasant substance that serves to repel enemies.

The lice do not willingly submit to the ants, and sometimes this is just as well. Many ants are not accustomed
to plant lice, and even those that are do not take to all
species. When we bring strange species together surprising things may happen. I once gave some aphids to some
Italian *Pheidole* ants. At first the hungry workers avoided
the unknown animals; in the end the ants overcame
their revulsion, and the plant lice were thrown to the
larvae, which ate them just as they did other insects
(cf. Fig. 5 a).

Experiments with other ants proved still more interesting. In Capri, I took some plant lice from a pine forest that had previously been visited by carpenter ants
(*Camponotus*) and set them down before *Acantholepis*
desert ants. The desert ants, usually quick to attack, at
first recoiled in fright. But the plant louse behaved as
usual when approached by an ant: it raised the tip of its
abdomen and excreted a drop of honey. The *Acantholepis*
immediately sucked up the drop. When the source dried
up, however, the ant was not satisfied. It pinched the
louse's abdomen, and when the frightened louse tried
to run away that was the end of it. The ant seized the
louse, crushed it, and proceeded to devour the meat
after the dessert! (See Fig. 42 c.) In several other cases
the lice were attacked and killed after they had provided
their drops of honey, and fellow ants were sometimes
alerted to help drag the carcass to the nest.

Not all the *Acantholepis* ants behaved in this way.
Some appeared to be accustomed to plant lice, and in-

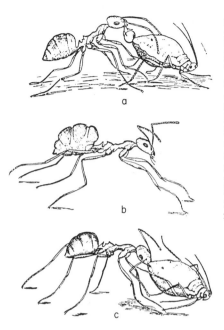

a

b

c

FIG. 42 *a-c. a*) *Acantholepis* ant, unaccustomed to plant lice, recoils a little and examines the stranger. The plant louse gives off a drop of honey. *b*) An *Acantholepis* ant that has filled its crop full of honey hastens home without killing the plant lice. *c*) The ant has licked up the exuded drop of honey, but is not satisfied. It seizes the plant louse, tugs it back and forth, kills it, and finally carries it home to the nest.

terestingly enough, this acquaintance must have begun quite recently. The pine trees that supported the pine aphids had been planted in Capri, along the Via Krupp, only a few years before. The *Acantholepis* ants visited these lice regularly and treated the bestowers of honey more gently than did the ants described above, which hailed from a faraway nest. This acquaintance has sprung up almost under our eyes, and the same process has gone on with the Argentine ants (*Iridomyrmex humilis*). These immigrants, now everywhere on the ascendant, have thoroughly accustomed themselves to the European plant lice, which cannot be known to them instinctively.

Another set of experiments casts further light on the relations between ants and aphids. Little flies, which under normal conditions an ant will immediately drag away to eat, were coated with foul-tasting aloes juice or a similar substance and a drop of honey was stuck to their hind ends. The most varied species of ants behaved in exactly the same way toward these "artificial aphids": they sucked up the drop of sugar and left the bitter fly in peace. If the ants were very hungry for meat, they sometimes overcame their revulsion, as we have seen that they will do with genuine plant lice. Finally, ants which normally visit plant lice were given little flies coated only with honey. If the flies were coated with sufficient liquid, or if new honey was added, the ants sucked themselves full of honey and ran home without taking the flies. But if they were not satisfied when the honey was exhausted, they killed the flies or dragged them off to be killed at the nest.

These observations and experiments give us an idea of how ants not yet habituated to plant lice form a relationship with them. Their unpleasant secretions protect the lice against any ants that are not too hungry, and since under normal circumstances they give off a great deal of honey—enough to fill an ant's crop—there is slight danger of their being eaten. This danger is, however, never wholly absent: even garden ants, which are very much habituated to their cows, are often seen carrying away dead or half-dead lice.

"But we often see plant lice protected by enclosures of earth, and we see the ants defending their cattle from attack." Both observations are accurate. Ants also build enclosures around a large drop of jam, and any bees or flies that approach it are bitten or sprayed with poison and chased away. The ants may also build walls around flowers that provide abundant nectar for a long time.

The same species that keep plant lice have a habit of making a circle around new food supplies of any sort, and impregnating them with their nest smell; in this way, as we shall see below, the ants incorporate the food in the nest territory. On occasion they build walls around this new territory. The ants proceed in exactly the same way with the plant lice, which to them are just another source of honey. Ants have no understanding of cause and effect, as we may observe when the "cattle" are attacked. On such occasions the ants, thinking that the attacks are directed against themselves, often kill the plant lice.

We have had to correct certain all-too-human notions about the ants' cattle raising, but it cannot be denied that in certain instances we really have a settled mutual relationship between the ants and the aphids. Certain timid little brown ants (*Lasius bruneus*) which dwell in hiding in the bark of trees have close ties with the large aphids of the genus *Stomaphis* that inhabit the same bark. If we break off the bark and uncover the nest, *Lasius bruneus* actually rescues its "cattle." This is no easy matter, for the aphid sinks its trunk, which is longer than its body, deep into the tree; the ant has quite a struggle pulling it out. The louse also seems to depend very heavily on the *Lasius* ants; in any case, it has never been found alone. Still, it is not quite accurate to say it cannot pour forth its sweet juice unless it is caressed by an ant.

There is a close relationship also between the yellow *Lasius flavus,* mentioned earlier, and certain root aphids. It has been established that in case of an attack this ant will rescue the lice as well as their brood as if they were its own. The yellow ants do in the strictest sense raise domestic animals. In consequence, they rarely have to leave their hill, and we seldom see them unless we uncover their nests, on purpose or by accident. The yellow ants cannot, however, depend on the aphids alone. According to actual counts at the Breslau Zoological Institute, nests with 25,000 to 50,000 workers, and 4,000 to 7,000 larvae and pupae, contained only five to 55 aphids —that is, in some cases only one louse for every 10,000 ants! The yellow ants also feed on the fungi growing on plant roots, though they do not cultivate them.

Experiments with ants that have not yet become wholly dependent on their "cattle" reveal how this mutual dependency develops, and show that firmly ingrained instincts can co-operate closely with learning ability.

The Way Out and Back

There is a wrong but persistent notion that the society
of the ants is a reflection of pure wisdom where all is ruled
by law and order. But when we look at a large nest, and
trust in what we see, there is no law and order: there

FIG. 43 *a*. Entrance to a nest of *Messor barbarus* in Capri (from
a photograph).

is only a great number of ants running about in wild confusion. We watch an individual ant: its behavior often
seems to have no rhyme or reason. Mark Twain was led
to conclude that ants are "the dumbest of all animals."

To gain an idea of how all the swarming and bustling
in an anthill comes about, we first must observe the be-

havior of a single ant—and not just for a moment but for a long time. With a little patience we can mark the abdomen or thorax of a few individuals with white, red, yellow, or green spots. Five colors and two combinations are enough to give different identifying marks to 35 individuals.

The harvester ants are particularly suited for such an observation. They include the European species (genus *Messor*) described in the Bible as seed gatherers, and

FIG. 43 *b*. A simple artificial nest for observing and photographing ants: a glass bowl covered with a sheet of cardboard or heavy paper. The ants in the bowl can climb up on the cardboard through the hole. The nest is set in a large dish of water to keep the ants from escaping.

several American species (genus *Pogonomyrmex*) of very similar habits. Among the harvesters, one set of workers finds and gathers the grain, another group husks and processes it (Figs. 32, 33, and 35). The South American leafcutters also have different work teams to bring in the leaves and to prepare them (Fig. 37 *a* and *b*). Our native ants, on the other hand, fill their crops to empty them only gradually inside the nest; in other words, they are out of sight much longer. Besides, they eat while they are inside, and this changes their behavior, for a sated animal differs in its actions from a hungry one.

The structure of the harvesters' nests also favors our purposes; they live in shafts dug between lumps of sand and blocks of stone and come out of their homes by way of vertical openings (cf. Fig. 43 *a*). Here they deposit their refuse, including their dead (Fig. 27).

It is very little trouble to set up an artificial *Messor* nest in a bowl. The outside world is represented by a piece of cardboard across the top, with a hole in the middle for a door (Fig. 43 *b*). From their native steppes and deserts, the ants are accustomed to bright sunlight, so that it is relatively easy to photograph them on the cardboard. In Fig. 44 *a*, a *Messor* ant is emerging for the first time from such an artificial nest. In Fig. 44 *b*, it runs in a loop around the entrance hole, to slip back into the nest. Such orientation trips are typical of all ants. They serve to explore first the immediate vicinity, then the more distant surroundings of the nest (Fig. 44 *g*). On later excursions, after the ant has come to know the neighborhood, it may at times rush back to the door of the nest, but without entering— just making sure, so to speak, that all is well. That is what happens in the ant's third sortie in Fig. 44 *g*.

By and by, the ant extends its knowledge of the neighborhood. It does not register every detail, but only notes such conspicuous features as a stone, a clump of grass, and the like, which it uses to get its bearings; it hurries toward such a point, only to start off in a different direction after it gets there (Fig. 45). Different individuals may pick out different road markers, or may bypass an obstacle in different ways (Fig. 67). Nor do ants always return by the same route by which they left the nest (cf. Figs. 67 and 68)—the number of possible variations is astounding.

Different species orient themselves in different ways. Some that are endowed with relatively good eyesight go largely by the position of the sun, as a special experiment shows (Fig. 46). An ant (*Lasius niger*) is moving across

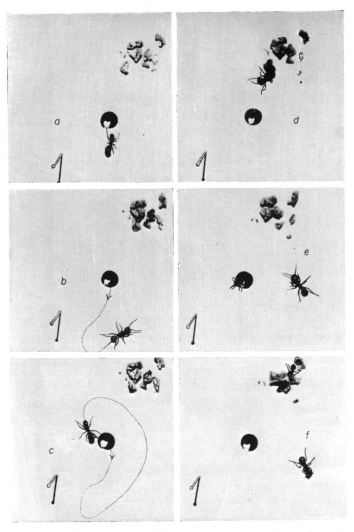

FIG. 44 *a-h*. Harvester ants (*Messor barbarus*) scouting. The ants were photographed on a sheet of paper covering an artificial nest, as in Fig. 43 *b,* on which their itineraries were then traced. In Fig. 44 *a* an ant leaves the nest, moves in a loop (*b*), and returns to the nest (*c*). Fig. 44 *g* shows the next three excursions of the same individual. On the third trip it follows for a time the edge of the paper; ants like to use such guide lines. At the end of the third trip the ant does not return into the nest but only to the entrance hole, and immediately starts on a new arc which brings

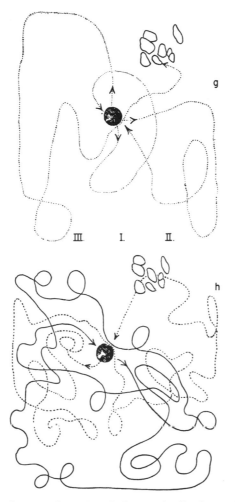

it to the food set out for it (crushed grains). *d*) The ant has found the food and carries back a grain. The nest is alerted, two companions appear—one large, one small—and start an excited search (*e*). Their itineraries differ greatly from those of ants that have not been alerted; compare *g* (before the alert) and *h* (after the alert). Each ant searches by itself. The small one finally finds the food (*h* dotted line). *f*) The large one, which can plainly be seen to feel the ground with its antennae, does not reach the food, and returns home (*h* solid line).

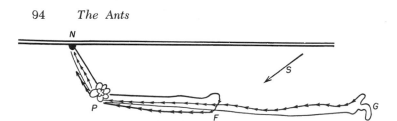

FIG. 45. Itineraries of a *Messor* ant identified by a spot of color, from the nest entrance N at the foot of a wall, to food (G) situated some ten feet away. First, the ant aims for the stalk of a leafy plant (P), and from there in an almost straight line at some clumps of grass (G). It now returns to the nest with a grass seed. All sorties follow the same route. On one occasion food is found at F. The arrow S indicates the rays of the sun, which also act as guides.

a stretch of sand directly toward the sun. We cover it with a box (x in Fig. 46). After two hours, the ant is released, and now starts at once on the return journey. But its line of march deviates by 30° from the route by which it came —exactly as many degrees as the sun has moved during the ant's two-hour captivity. This interesting experiment was repeated many times with various periods of imprisonment. The angle in the ant's paths always corresponded to the change in the position of the sun, with only slight variations. Frisch's studies of bees have shown that the social insects orient themselves largely by polarized light. The most recent observations leave no doubt that the same is true of the ants.

Such experiments are, of course, not always successful. They fail on uneven ground with many possible points of orientation such as trees, bushes, and weeds. They also fail with the ants that have the best eyesight (*Formica*). These ants, even on their long journeys, note certain large images such as a big tree, or a house beyond or near the nest, and take their bearings from these. The so-called light compass or sun compass is only one means of orientation among many.

The kind of soil and, by implication, the sense of touch

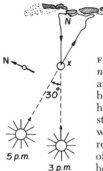

FIG. 46. So-called light compass. An ant (*Lasius niger*) started from nest N toward the sun and arrived at x. Here it was covered with a dark box and held captive. When it was released two hours later, the ant ran home with the sun straight behind it. But since the sun had meanwhile moved 30° to the left, the ant did not reach the nest entrance but a point to the right of it. It then scouted until it found the way home.

also play a part. An ant may note, for instance, that a stretch of sand is followed by a forest floor with pine needles after which there comes a smooth stony surface. Scents also are important. If the sequence of soils or smells in a familiar itinerary is changed, the ant grows uncertain at once. It begins to scout again in loops until it hits upon something that is familiar. In short, it takes a number of impressions to make sure of a successful return.

It is amazing how far a scout ant will travel, and how well it knows the way home. Once, near Naples in Italy, I offered a bread crumb to a *Messor* ant. The animal at once proceeded to take it home. It had to travel more than twenty feet as the crow flies, and climb over a six-foot wall. All this it did without hesitation, and without any help from other ants—sure proof that it knew its way perfectly.

No wonder such feats gave rise to the notion that ants, as well as bees and termites, are drawn back to the nest by some mysterious magnetic force. But a great number of exact experiments have shown that what enables the insects to find the way is in fact their memory. Even a slight shift in the accustomed conditions may provoke the ant to new exploratory gyrations until it discovers

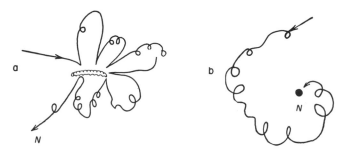

FIG. 47 *a-b*. *a*) Itinerary of an alerted desert ant (*Dorymyrmex goetschi*). The ant finds a victim (caterpillar) and "dances" around, returning again and again to the prey. *b*) *Dorymyrmex* returning home to alarm the nest (N).

something familiar. As a rule it will do so fairly soon. But we also find ants running about in utter confusion very close to their nest, and ultimately coming to grief because they cannot find the way home. Scouting ants, like human explorers, may fall victims to their profession.

The ants' scouting trips are like our scientific explorations in still another way: they open up new resources. Sooner or later, one of the scouts finds something that may be of value. The new, unknown object is carefully examined. The manner of examination is a matter of temperament: some ants, such as the hunter ants (*Myrmica*), approach cautiously, while others, impetuous, such as the Chilean desert ants, charge wildly (cf. Fig. 47). The discoverer usually recoils a few times, or may even take flight if the new object seems dangerous. If the object turns out to be of no interest, the exploration is soon resumed. But if the discovery is useful, the ant attempts at once to carry it off, alone if possible, even if it should take more than one trip.

Some species practice division of labor: the find is carried only part way to the nest. Harvester ants, for example, set up grain depots all along the route. Other species turn the liquid in their crop over to nest companions who carry it home—such co-operation among ants raises the question: how do ants recognize their nest mates?

Recognition and Communication

To form a community and to act in concert, we human beings need some way to recognize and communicate with each other. Men know each other by their common language, by uniforms, or by badges. They communicate by password, gesture, or in writing. Their distress call may be a shriek of fear or an S O S signal. We have innumerable ways—and nearly all of them are addressed to the eye or to the ear.

Ants must rely on different means. For one thing, some species have no eyes, and none of them seem to have ears. It is at best doubtful whether their own chirping or knocking sounds are perceived as sound; perhaps they note them only as vibrations, only as movement. Ants communicate through other senses, particularly through smell. Their organs of smell are mainly in their antennae. Their smell provides them with a badge of recognition—they may be said to wear a scent uniform.

This uniform consists of the species smell and the nest smell. Each nest, even of the same species, has a slightly different smell, due to a difference in the surroundings. Anyone who does not smell like a member of the colony will as a rule be taken for an enemy—not excluding members of the same species from another nest.

The smell uniform and its effects have been studied closely. First, we eliminated the means of recognition. If you blindfold a man and plug his ears, he will have difficulty recognizing his friends. The same happens to ants whose antennae are coated with varnish so as to plug up the tiny organs of smell. They behave differently, according to temperament—either furiously attacking all comers including their nest mates, or living peacefully even among enemies.

We have also succeeded in changing the scent uniform: we killed and squashed a number of ants, and bathed ants of another colony in the liquid. Ants belonging to the same colony as the victims were at first deceived, though they remained distrustful. But as the scent wore off, they became increasingly hostile.

We also tried it the other way around: we changed the smell of certain ants so that their nest mates thought them to be enemies. Even protracted separation often engenders a certain distrust, especially if the different groups are kept in artificial nests of different materials, such as plaster containers and glass tubes (Figs. 65 and 66). I once separated the inhabitants of a *Messor* nest and fed one group chiefly on meat (insects and the like), the other only on seeds. After two to three months their scents had grown so different that the two groups engaged in the wildest battle I have ever seen among this normally peace-loving species. They could no longer bear each other's smell.

Alert Signals

How do ants communicate with one another? Let us go back to the *Messor* ant which went foraging in Fig. 44. On the third sortie it found food (Fig. 44 *d*). In nature the food would be a ripe stalk of grass, or a pile of seeds—in our experiments it is a pile of crushed grain. If it is a small pile, the ant carries it off grain by grain. If it is familiar with the road, our harvester will move approximately in a straight line.

But if a large amount is discovered, the finder becomes extremely excited and communicates this excitement to any nest mates it meets, particularly those that are not engaged in some other activity. The finder usually does what it can to get the idle companions going, by striking them with its antennae or even its legs, at times even by butting them in the side with its head. The companions so treated grow excited, too; they rush from the nest and begin to search. Their itineraries show that they are far more excited than the first scouts (cf. Fig. 44 *g-h*); their gyrations are smaller and more intricate. Among the livelier species, the alerted ants spurt out of the nest in all directions like buckshot—and like buckshot, only a few hit the mark. Those who find the food supply begin at once to carry in the grains and to spread the word. Little by little the number of gatherers at the food site increases. Those that have failed to find the food return to the nest and quiet down (cf. Fig. 44 *g*), unless they are caught up in a new horde emerging from the nest.

How does this alarm work? Among most species

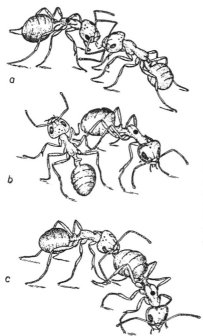

FIG. 48 *a-c.* Meeting between two workers of the
garden ant (*Lasius emarginatus*). *a*) The left-hand
ant (marked with color
spot) alerts its nest mate
which is heading toward it.
b-c) The alerted ant turns
around and follows the
other.

studied, it has three progressive stages that blend into
one another. The first is a more or less intense pecking of
the body; the alerted ant responds with only a slight motion. This form of alarm is used by some ants to inform
the nurses of some change, and to prompt them to move
eggs and larvae. The second stage may still be a pecking
of thorax or abdomen, but includes besides, blows with
the antennae, the forelegs, and the head. This is the way
in which a finder of food summons help when his find is
too large for a single ant.

Some livelier species show still another kind of motion. They may put their legs down in a particular way,
or even cross them in a kind of dance, and dart about in
circles or wavy lines. Such dances (also known among

FIG. 49. Soldier of a *Messor*
ant after danger alarm.

the bees) vary slightly from species to species. Compare the paths of the ants in Figs. 47, 61, 62, and 63.

The excitement of the finder grows with the size of its find, and may reach the third stage. While the gentler ways of communicating excitement make no impression on ants busy with some other task, the highest degree— the danger signal—sets the whole nest in motion. At the danger signal, most ants run about in high excitement, their jaws open (Fig. 49); some raise their abdomen almost straight up (Fig. 50), and often give off a drop of poison from its tip. At first the alarmed ants behave like those that gave the alarm; then they usually take up some work that is at hand. Only those that happen to get to the source of the alarm can fight a possible enemy. Others, finding themselves near food stores or the brood, may start their carrying; still others may fall to repairing a crumbling part of the nest. Now confusion is complete. But if nothing further happens the alarm soon subsides, and the ants return to their earlier labors.

All observations so far show that the alert signal has no descriptive content but merely transmits a state of excitement. What the alarmed ants will do depends on other stimuli. Various experiments have shown the alarm message says nothing about either the place or the nature of what caused it. Ants excited by a food alert pick up any food they come across, and carry it off. Some orientation may be provided by the relay habit among the harvesters: the finders of a seed supply soon stop carrying their booty all the way to the nest; they put it down at convenient spots, and soon the road is marked by little food depots. Alerted ants that come across one of these piles carry it off, and when the pile is exhausted they keep on looking from depot to depot until at last they get to the real source.

Similar relay is practiced among the ants that forage for liquid food. The finders pump their crops and stomachs full. They stop in sheltered spots, or else they may regurgitate their liquid and transmit it to some nest mate idling near the nest. Like a relay racer passing on his staff, the nest mate will proceed to the nest to disgorge the food—or else to wait there, a living depot, for the arrival of a new ant to which it can transfer the nectar.

FIG. 50. On receiving danger alarm the Chilean *Camponotus morosus* raises its abdomen.

Trail Making

Some species of ants, especially those that feed on dead animals, go much further in co-operation. They make a trail which allows the alerted ants to find the source of food without delay. The alert says nothing about the place of the food, but the way to it is laid out.

How it is done can best be observed with Mediterranean *Pheidole* and the American *Solenopsis* species, which feed mostly on meat. These ants drag small corpses into the nest whenever possible, or else rapidly dissect them and carry off the pieces. Unlike the harvesters, these ants come to each other's aid at once if the prey is too large for one to carry.

The film strips in Fig. 51 show the progress of a food alert among the *Pheidole:* A fly is stuck with a pin to a piece of paper. (The shadow of the pin and of the camera-stand serve as a sun clock to show how fast the whole thing takes place.) In Fig. 51 *a*, the fly has not yet been discovered. At length a scout (Fig. 51 *b*) reaches the fly. A little later, a second scout appears. The two attempt to drag away the fly; they fail, and run home and give the alert. Unfortunately, we have not yet been able to film an alert among the *Pheidole* ants for it takes place deep within the nest. But the result of alarm is striking enough. Most of the eight to ten ants which at first come from the nest reach the prey (Fig. 51 *c*). They, too, are unable to tear off the fly, and run home to give a new alarm. A new troop of alerted ants appears (Fig.

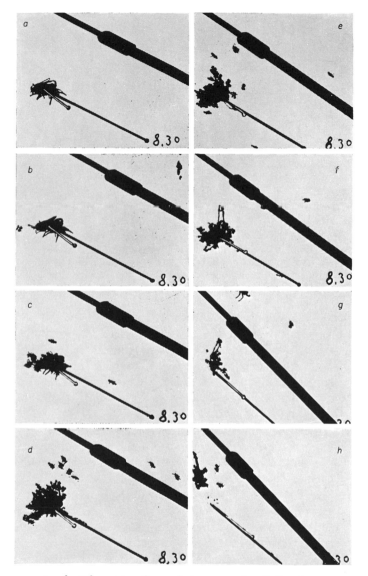

FIG. 51 *a-h*. Film strip of an alert among the Italian house ant (*Pheidole pallidula*). Explanation in the text. The shadow of the pin on which the fly is spitted serves as a sun clock, indicating the time elapsed since the beginning of the experiment (8:30 o'clock).

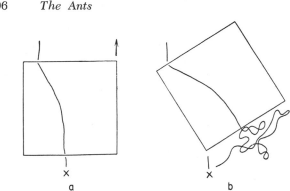

FIG. 52 *a-b*. *a*) A *Pheidole* ant, hurrying home across a sheet of paper from food (at x) to the nest, has laid a trail along which the alerted ants run toward the food. *b*) The paper is turned, and the alerted ants follow the trail to the edge of the paper. Here they start scouting again to find the food.

51 *d*)—how quickly is shown by the shadow of the pin: it has scarcely moved.

All of them now set to work tugging at the fly (Fig. 51 *e-f*). They tear off some pieces, which they at once carry home (Fig. 51 *g*). At length nothing remains but the fly's trunk, which is likewise torn from the pin and dragged home (Fig. 51 *h*).

A dead worm or lizard is handled in the same way. The alerted ants find their way to the food quickly because the finder lays a scent trail. We shall watch him on his way home to see how he does it.

The ant presses its body against the ground, so that it can make only slow uneven progress in spite of its great excitement. The pressure imparts some of the ant's smell to the ground: this is the trail the alerted ants will follow. They may not follow it exactly; sometimes they take detours, or temporarily lose the scent. If so, they begin to search for the trail and, having found it, follow it to the food.

Although the trail laid by a single finder does not last long—with *Pheidole* ants only about six minutes—it serves to guide the first group of alerted ants. If they are unable to carry the prey by themselves, they run home, refreshing the trail. The result is a well-marked trail often many feet in length. A mass of ants may soon swarm about where a moment before there were none.

The presence of trails can be proved in many different ways. For example: we set a sheet of paper between nest and food; the finder lays a trail across it (Fig. 52 *a*). The paper is pivoted, and now the ants start exploratory spirals where the trail breaks off, as they do whenever they come into unknown territory (Fig. 52 *b*). If they

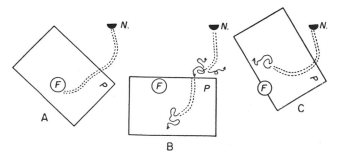

FIG. 53 *A-C*. Turntable experiments showing how the Chilean ant *Solenopsis gayi* lays its trail. N = nest entrance, P = pivot on which the rectangular paper is turned, F = food, which remains in the same position and at the same distance from the nest. *A*) An ant has found the food and returns home, giving the alert and marking the trail (double dotted line). New ants appear, follow the trail, and find the food. *B*) After the finder's return home, the paper is turned and the trail broken. Three ants emerge, follow the trail, and start exploratory loops where it breaks off. One ant recovers the trail on the sheet of paper, follows it, runs past the food, and at the end of the trail explores the piece of paper. *C*) The paper is turned again. The trail on the paper now connects with the trail off the paper. The ants follow the trail, run past the food, and explore at the end of the trail. (The same experiments were also made with artificial trails.)

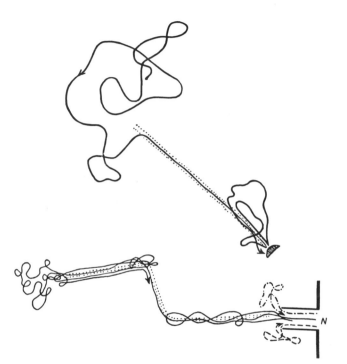

FIGS. 54 and 55. Artificial trail of the Chilean ant *Solenopsis gayi*.
FIG. 54. An artificial trail is made on paper with the abdomen of
a *Solenopsis* worker. An ant of the same colony is caught near
another entrance to the nest and placed on the paper. It scouts;
as soon as it finds the trail, it follows it to the nest entrance, recoils
from the strange situation, scouts, finds the trail again, and finally
runs into the nest.
FIG. 55. A trail (double dotted line) is made with the abdomen
of an ant on a sheet of paper outside an artificial nest (N). Two
workers emerge from the nest (broken lines), fail to find the trail,
and after exploratory loops return to the nest. A third ant finds
the artificial trail and follows it for some distance. It returns to
the nest, and then follows the trail again, this time to the end.
There it scouts for a while and then follows the artificial trail back
to the nest. (For technical reasons the ant's path is sometimes
marked not on, but to the side of the trail.)

happen back on the trail, they again follow it—even if it leads them past the food (Fig. 53 *b* and *c*).

With certain species (*Pheidole, Solenopsis*), we succeeded in creating trails artificially. We rubbed the bodies of freshly killed ants over a sheet of paper, making a trail which the alerted ants followed just as if a finder ant had laid it (Figs. 54 and 55). The same kind of trail made with a dead grasshopper or fly has no such effect (Fig. 56).

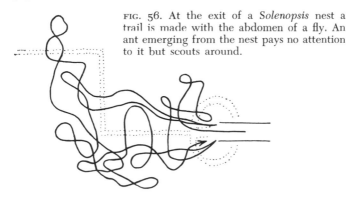

FIG. 56. At the exit of a *Solenopsis* nest a trail is made with the abdomen of a fly. An ant emerging from the nest pays no attention to it but scouts around.

Experiments with artificial trails also revealed exactly how the ant lays its trails. The ant does not use the formic acid in the poison gland of its more or less developed sting mechanism. This acid is the danger signal which throws the alarmed ants into high excitement (Fig. 57). Other glands serve to lay trails. Their secretion gives the ant scent that at times is even perceptible to us.

The scent trail of the ants might be compared with the trail made by the exhaust gases of an automobile. Fig. 58 shows an unusually large gland, found in certain species, connected to something like an exhaust pipe. Such pictures gave me the idea for still another experiment. I put a number of ants into a small syringe. After they had filled it with their scent, I used the syringe to

FIG. 57. Artificial trails before a *Pheidole* nest. On a sheet of paper a trail represented by the double dotted line was daubed with the abdomens of five dead *Pheidole* ants. At the upper black dot, a large drop of poison dripped from the stinger of a dead ant, at the lower dot a smaller one. Two alerted ants are placed on the trail. They follow it to the first drop of poison; there they run about wildly, as they would at the danger signal. They quiet down, find the trail again and continue as far as the second drop, where the excitement recurs.

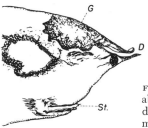

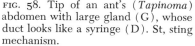

FIG. 58. Tip of an ant's (*Tapinoma*) abdomen with large gland (G), whose duct looks like a syringe (D). St, sting mechanism.

produce an artificial trail. Under favorable conditions, alerted ants followed such a trail even better than that laid by a finder ant, presumably because it contained the concentrated body scent of a large number of *Formica* ants and was consequently stronger than that of a single individual.

When ants travel the same road many times they may produce lasting scent trails. The ants leave droppings along such a road, which in the end actually becomes visible. I found such trails around *Lasius* colonies in Carinthia, and was able to observe them year after year. They usually lead from a nest whose immediate vicinity is exhausted, to distant sources of supply. Well-ordered traffic develops on such a highway. The ants follow it from the nest in an unbroken line; at the end of the road, they fan out. On the way back they gather again and return to the nest in a column along the highway. An interruption of such a trail produces impressive traffic jams which take time to straighten out.

Roads of this sort made over a piece of paper allow us to throw "switches" (as in the turntable experiments, Fig. 53) without any change in the behavior of the ants.

FIG. 59 *a-c.* A bridge leads from an "ant island" (a nest surrounded by a moat) of *Formica sanguinea,* to two feeding places *a*). Results of an alert issuing at 12:30 o'clock from the right-hand source of food: *c*) the right-hand food source is heavily occupied by ants, *b*) the left-hand one remains deserted.

However, there is a limit which varies with the species. Homeward-bound workers, particularly, are likely to be disturbed if the trail is turned too much, as in Fig. 60. In this experiment, members of the genus *Cremastogaster* are returning to their nest in the direction of the arrow, along a trail on a sheet of paper. When the sheet of paper is turned by 35°, the ants follow the trail to the end and return to it after losing it. When it is turned by 55°, most of the ants are quick to note that something is wrong and turn back; when it is turned by 75°, none of

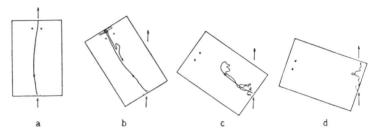

a   b   c   d

FIG. 60 *a-d*. Turntable experiments with a well-established road of *Cremastogaster scutellaris*. For explanation see text.

them follows the trail (Fig. 60 *c* and *d*). They reorient themselves, and slowly find their way to the nest.

What does this mean? Let us think of it in this way: the ants hurrying home have a definite goal in view— the nest. We have seen (Fig. 45) that they hold their course by aiming at intermediate goals. When they are not following a trail they orient themselves exclusively in that way. If there is a trail, their attention flags. They trot along the trail, where the going is easier, and begin to disregard the customary points of orientation, growing visibly more careless. They will follow a trail as long as the points of orientation are not shifted too much. But they will take notice when the shift is excessive, and leave the trail. With ants hurrying away from the nest at an alert, it is a different matter; they have no definite goal in view. Now the shift can be much greater. They race along the trail because they have been alerted and expect something at the end of it.

Sightless ants and termites depend on trails entirely. Besides their smell they have only their sense of touch, which responds to changes less readily than does sight.

The better their eyesight, the less effective the scent trail. To ants of the genus *Formica,* scent trails are secondary; they orient themselves more by the position of the sun (Fig. 46) and other visual markers. Even among these, an ant that has found a source of food may

FIG. 61. The garden ant (*Lasius emarginatus*) runs home giving the alert.

lead its nest mates to it by a trail (Fig. 59), and if the trail is blurred, confusion arises. If, for example, we cover the trail with sand the ants that have been alerted cannot find their way to the food supply. Often, the finder does not go home at all, but simply circles around the food it has discovered. In this way it stakes a claim to the territory (Fig. 62), and so impregnates it with its own smell that nest mates which have been alerted, or which come to the spot on scouting parties of their own, are immediately attracted. As we have seen, we find something similar in the aphid-tending species.

There is another interesting phenomenon, which we have discovered just recently: the use of a scent trail by ants belonging to entirely different species or genera from those that laid it. The *Cremastogaster* ants produce a very distinct scent trail—and this trail is also used by the

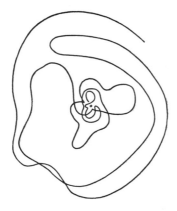

FIG. 62. Path of an ant (*Cam-ponotus distinguendus*) giving the alert.

FIG. 63. *Acantholepis frauenfeldi* runs home giving the alert.

FIG. 64. See text.

similarly colored *Camponotus lateralis*. Experiments have shown how this comes about: I succeeded in accustoming *Camponotus lateralis* to artificial trails, which I made with a brush dipped in formic acid or formalin, between their nest and a food supply. At first they took no interest in this trail. After a while they found it of help and formed the habit of using it, even when I made experiments such as are shown in Figs. 52 and 53, rotating the paper bearing the artificial trail. In the same way, observations in nature have shown, *Camponotus lateralis* gradually learns to make use of the trail of *Cremastogaster*.

The paths of searching ants and their scent trails may often seem to us confused and absurd. Why, for instance, are the itineraries in Figs. 62 and 63 so twisted? Mark Twain would perhaps have regarded them as one more proof of the ants' stupidity. But if he had said such a thing about Fig. 64, he would have blundered: it is not the itinerary of an ant but an Alpine road photographed from the air. Seen from above, some human activities might well seem absurd to an observer who does not have the key to the puzzle.

Body Form and Division of Labor

What sort of ants sally forth to explore the unknown, alert their nest mates, and make roads?

In the nest, we know, there is a queen; at times there are males; there are workers of different ages and often different sizes; and there may be soldiers. Which ants lead the scouting expeditions, and which ants follow? Which ants remain in the nest with the brood?

The males, we have seen, are not the leaders. Their only function is to fertilize the young females in the marriage flight. The queen has no time to direct outside activities. She is solely occupied with laying as many eggs as possible and increasing the population; she is confined to the nest—her work is definitely domestic.

This leaves only the workers and soldiers of different age classes. One is tempted to attribute the role of leader to the soldiers. But to repeat, the soldiers are not particularly warlike or aggressive. The name merely indicates that they have a special body form different from that of the other workers; usually their heads are larger than normal, sometimes as large or even larger than the queen's head. But these giant skulls hamper the soldiers in certain activities such as the care of the fungus gardens or of the eggs and the youngest larvae. There is little they can do in the nest, and as an unemployed ant, after a brief resting period, always looks for work, we often find the big-heads of some species outside the nest. More of them than of the small workers venture out into the world; they go scouting, bring in new-found booty, and are thus on hand to resist attacks on the nest. This holds true for the harvesters and particularly the fungus growers, among which the division of labor is most highly developed. Among these species, certain of the many transitional forms between workers and soldiers seem at times even to be favored for specific outside activities. Among other species, no such division of outside labor is discernible—in general, the division of labor according to size must always be taken only as a dominant tendency, not as a strict law. Some activities are carried on not only by the favored size but by other sizes as well. Thus big-heads for example may be found at home, building or caring for the eggs, larvae, and pupae.

If the big-heads prefer outside work, it is usually because they are less persevering than the other workers and never stay very long at any one activity. It may be that they have difficulty carrying their big skulls around, and tire more quickly than do the other workers; of this we cannot be certain, although it seems likely. The "shiftiness" of the soldiers has often been demonstrated statistically for the grain-collecting *Messor* species. In one experiment, two small workers made 547 grain-carrying trips in 20 hours; in the same period, two soldiers made only 34 such trips, although they kept running in and out. In another experiment, seven soldiers changed activity 19 times in ten days, seven small workers only three times.

This unsteadiness also explains why a nest containing only soldiers raises its brood poorly or not at all, even though the soldiers, too, are females. As we shall see, they are in fact closer to the genuine females than are the smaller forms that often show great perseverance in their labor.

But the very steadiness of the medium-sized and smaller workers can produce inefficiency: individuals wholly devoted to building activity keep removing the earth from the nest as long as it is sufficiently damp—they keep on until the nest collapses. Another example of pointless activity may be observed if we set up a colony composed exclusively of small workers and a large brood: despite the most diligent care, the number of larvae and eggs diminishes, since the workers often prefer to eat the brood rather than leave the nest even for nearby food.

Apart from size, there is also a physiological basis for the division of labor. The callows remain in the nest and immediately take over the care of the brood. They may make their change-over to another activity at various times. If there is a large brood to be cared for, the young ants stay home longer; if the brood is small, they shift to other work relatively early. As we have said, an ant cannot stay idle for long; if the services of a younger worker are no longer needed by the brood, it soon turns to something else.

An unemployed young worker usually begins by looking on, so to speak, while another group is working. It may run along part of the way with a group that is hauling building material or grain from chamber to chamber; finally, as though in play, it lends a hand, and then keeps on working. As a matter of fact, older unemployed ants join working parties in the same way.

There is often another occupation, halfway between domestic and outside activity, and that is sentry duty. The young unemployed worker who is about to leave the nest stops near the entrance. The urge to go out is counterbalanced by the fear of the unknown. Once this fear is overcome, the worker begins little by little to explore the outside world. But it is not only the young ants that act as sentries; this function is confined to no particular age group.

The division of labor among ants reminds us of the bees, which also must perform a variety of tasks—care of the brood, building of cells, defense of the hive, foraging. Among the bees, too, different age groups perform different activities. There are no lifelong builders and nurses, sentries, and food collectors; each worker bee performs all these labors successively—a system very different from that of the human community.

For the bees the reason is known: the different activities depend on physical development. Only young workers can feed the brood, because only they possess the necessary salivary and feeding glands. After ten to twenty days, these glands atrophy, and the wax glands in the abdomen develop instead. The workers then busy themselves with building the comb. When the wax glands dry up after another twenty days, the workers, for the remainder of their life, turn into foragers, bringing in honey and pollen.

This dependence on the stages of physical development can be shown to exist among the ants as well. Only the young queen is able to raise a brood. If we take her first eggs away from her, she may attempt once or twice again to found a colony—how often varies with the species. But there always comes a time when she can no longer succeed. Even if she is kept under the best conditions and given ample food, her eggs fail to develop into adult workers—her feeding glands begin to shrivel. Similarly, young workers are better nurses than the old, although there is no such hard and fast law in the development of the ants as there is with the bees.

Size and physiology are not wholly sufficient to account for the division of labor. In a number of experiments we identified all of the individuals in a nest with little spots of color. If we keep track of the activities of these ants —as we have done with certain *Messor* ants for their entire life—we find that some individuals always prefer one specific form of work, even though none of the considerations advanced so far could account for their preference. In an attempt to find out whether the habits of such specialized workers could be changed, we established experimental nests composed of two groups of individuals, one adjusted to collecting, the other to nursing. The first group was supplied only with eggs and larvae, and given no opportunity to do anything else; the second was separated from the brood and put into a new nest where there was only cleaning and other such work to be done. In each case it took a good deal of time before the ants adapted themselves to the new work, but in one instance, some individuals were engaged in the new activity after only six days. Some remained faithful to their new labors after they were returned to their old nest and the opportunity to follow their original occupation; others returned to their favorite form of work. I made similar experiments with freshly captured ants; the results were the same. It follows that a preference for a specific activity must often be attributed to perseverance. At the beginning of its career the ant, for some reason, takes to a particular occupation and remains faithful to it as long as possible. Thus, totally different characters develop, as every careful observer of ants can testify.

These individual differences show that, in addition to body form and phase of development, a psychological factor is also involved in the division of labor. It largely accounts for the greater diversity of ant societies, in contrast to the more rigid development of the bees.

Despite their sometimes inappropriate behavior, insect societies often show to an astonishing degree that they are a unit, a single whole that is far more than an aggregate of many individuals. For example, in an experiment most of the builders were removed from a beehive: the remaining bees were incapable of preparing wax. A situation was then created in which it became urgent to build cells. And build cells they did—bees that had passed the age of wax-making, whose wax glands had collapsed and seemed empty. Fatty tissue with highly nutritive cells joined the shriveled wax glands, recharged them, so to speak, and, as microscopic examination showed, caused them to develop once again.

In other beehives, the colony was split up into two age groups. The younger group lacked the older workers that fly out to forage. Their food supply was soon exhausted, and after two days a number of them lay prostrate with hunger. But on the third day things took a new turn. Bees between one and two weeks of age flew out of the hive—they usually do so only at the age of about three weeks—and soon returned laden with food. Their fully developed feeding glands marked them as nurses; yet what was decisive was not their physiology but the needs of the community. The glands submitted to the situation and shriveled up within a few days.

The older group, on the other hand, lacked nurses. The gap was filled by the least aged among them, which retained their feeding glands far beyond the usual term.

In ant societies there is no such strict division of labor on the basis of physiology as there is among the bees. Still, a distinction may be made between the younger workers which do inside service and the older ones whose activities are carried on chiefly outside the nest. Although as a rule one group does not take up the activities of the other, this can happen in emergencies. In *Messor* nests that were artificially restricted to outside workers and a considerable brood, the eggs, larvae, and pupae were totally neglected, so that nearly all of them perished. In the end, however, the ants adapted themselves and began to care for the few surviving eggs. One-year-old workers were still acting as nurses, something that never happens in normal ant societies.

Further, we find this striking phenomenon among the ants (and the bees as well): if a state lacks a queen, workers often take her place. Usually these are workers that are closer to the genuine female, particularly soldiers or large workers, which, as we shall see, often represent intermediate forms between worker and queen (cf. Fig. 78). Such substitutes lay eggs, often in great numbers. In this way they meet the nursing instincts of their companions and postpone the decay of the colony —though they cannot prevent it. For their eggs, as we shall see, produce males which take no part in the work of the society.

Thus, bees and ants can do far more than most animals to protect their society from danger. One is tempted to say that their will governs their body. But unfortunately we know nothing about the will of the bees and ants. We must leave the riddle unsolved, and be content with the observation that an insect society often behaves like a single animal or human organism whose parts can do amazing things when the life of the whole is in danger.

The Mental Faculties

The individual differences among the members of an ant nest give rise to a question that was formerly in the forefront of discussion. What moves insect societies, reason or instinct? Both views found ardent adherents, and both camps produced evidence for their views. We still read accounts of ant behavior purporting to show how intelligent the ants are, what clever ways they have of getting into the groceries, and so on. Readers of this book will have little difficulty in accounting for most examples of this kind: some ant, during a long journey in search of food, finally ran across the provisions in question, sometimes in a hidden, almost inaccessible place, perhaps by crawling through a hole in the cupboard or by climbing up a string. The finder makes a trail and gives the alert, and soon the place where "there wasn't a trace of ants" is alive with them. The single scouting ant easily escaped attention.

In the same context belong the recurrent tales of the cleverness of ants escaping from vessels or artificial nests. It is true that they do cause the entomologist a good deal of trouble. Given time they will bore through any cork stopper of an observation tube (Fig. 65), through any of the walls of a plaster nest (Fig. 66). "It's the urge for freedom; they know they are shut up, and they have a will to leave their prison," we may be told with a special emphasis on will. At first sight this view seems justified— but if our prejudiced observer keeps on looking, he will see the ants, at the first sign of danger, scurrying back into a well set-up artificial nest. I used to start my *Pheidole* cultures in little tubes such as that shown in Fig. 65. Some ants would invariably escape, and it was always a delightful spectacle to see them hurry back to the tubes and disappear through the holes in the cork they had taken such pains to bore. If hungry ants are given food on the

FIG. 65. Artificial nest in a glass tube. The ants build their chambers among the pebbles and earth piled between pierced disks of cork. (Reduced by half.)

outside, they race "home" to the little tube or plaster nest to distribute it.

There are other examples. In one case, my ants had considerably broadened their "escape" hole. I was prepared for the worst, particularly because all sorts of nest building materials were piled up outside the opening. But as it turned out, the *Pheidole* had merely thrown their refuse out of the artificial nest. They themselves had remained inside, a sign that they were comfortable. On another occasion, I shut a few ants out of the nest by pasting up the hole they had made in the cork. Next day, the locked-out ants were busy gnawing through the cork from outside to get back into the nest.

Similar was the behavior of *Messor* ants in Majorca, and *Solenopsis* species in Chile, which I permitted to run from their plaster nests into their natural environment. They hurried into the open, across the terrace on which the nest was set up, to collect grains, seeds, or bread crumbs. To be sure, I had to wait at times for hours before they were all back, and occasionally one of them would get lost. These ants behaved like bees, which we can also keep in artificial nests if we meet their biological requirements. There are no grounds for regarding a well set-up artificial nest as a "dungeon" or its inhabitants as "prisoners"—they show no inclination to forsake the "security" of their man-made home.

Why, then, do they break out if they are comfortable in the artificial nest? It is simply because of the urge to enlarge their nest territory—the same urge that prompts them to break into things. Attempts to break out of the nest always begin in the same way: an unemployed ant starts to gnaw somewhere; if it makes good headway, it grows excited and infects other unemployed ants with its zeal. A team forms, just as when food is found, and the hole grows larger and larger. The time has come for the observer to be on the lookout—best by diverting the working zeal of the ants elsewhere. It often suffices to turn the nest; the ants then do not readily find their work site, and start doing something else.

Many examples can be given to show that such activity usually springs from an unsatisfied working urge, and not from any conscious will to escape. The gnawing and drilling may stop when there is only a little way left to go; or the ants may painstakingly drill a new hole right next to a broad passage from one chamber to an-

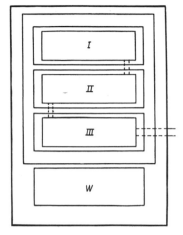

FIG. 66. Artificial ants' nest in a plaster block. Chambers I, II, and III are sealed off with strips of glass, and the whole is covered with a large glass plate. Sections II and III are darkened; a tube as in Fig. 65 may be joined with a glass pipe to Section III. There is also a water chamber, W; the water poured into it is distributed over the plaster block and moistens the chambers in varying degree (III is moistened most, II less, I very little), so that the ants may seek out the amount of dampness that suits them.

other in an artificial nest (Fig. 66), or next to a large hole in the cork disk of a tube (Fig. 65).

But do these seemingly pointless actions give us the right to call the ants, with Mark Twain, the "stupidest of animals"? By no means. It is often amazing what they can do. But we must take a different approach to the psychology of the ants, rather than judge their behavior by human standards, as Mark Twain did.

Let us look again at the ant which emerges for the first time from its nest and scouts about to get to know its surroundings (Fig. 44). We cannot help being amazed at how quickly such a creature learns. Once I put into my breast pocket a tube containing some tiny tropical *Tapinoma melanocephalum*, such as are often found in greenhouses, to take it to the laboratory. In the course of my journey, which took some three-quarters of an hour, the ants bored their way out of the tube and, as I noticed only later, began to swarm all over my jacket. But they had already explored this unfamiliar ground so thoroughly that they were able to hurry "home," that is, back to the tube in my breast pocket, as soon as they were alarmed.

I then devised a series of experiments which showed that within half an hour this small and exceedingly fast-moving ant can thoroughly "learn" an area some three feet in diameter, and "know" the situation of the nest entrance well enough to return to it in a straight line. Evidently, it learns—that is, forms lasting impressions—very quickly. The ant is not, as was formerly supposed, led to the nest entrance by some magical force. If the entrance is moved, the ant first looks in the spot where it used to be and only then begins to grow accustomed to the new situation. If there were some magnetic attraction, the change of location would make no difference. That we are in fact dealing with a process of learning and habituation, a linking (association) of experiences, is shown by the mistakes made by the ants under such conditions.

A large box or frame covered with a sheet of glass was connected with an artificial nest by means of a glass tube. Food was placed in the corner of the frame farthest from the nest (Fig. 67, F). Between the food and the nest entrance was placed an obstacle—a dark glass saucer (S) which the ants had to bypass on either side. A number of *Messor* ants were marked with colored spots, so that all could be closely watched. For some days ant No. 26, marked with a red spot on the thorax and a white spot on the abdomen, carried grains from the food source along the path marked I in Fig. 67. Another ant took the lower path shown in Fig. 67. We mention this only to show that different ants took different routes.

Then the obstacle, the black saucer, was pushed against the wall of the frame. Ant No. 26 was now compelled to make the difficult climb between bowl and wall (Fig. 68, II). On its next trip out, the ant visibly hesitated on approaching the saucer, and did not climb

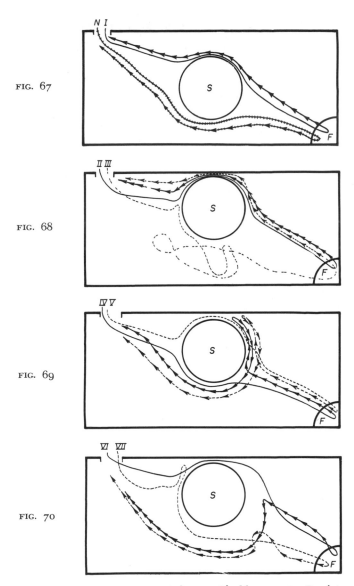

FIG. 67

FIG. 68

FIG. 69

FIG. 70

FIGS. 67-70. Memory tests carried out with *Messor* ants. Road to the food (F) without arrow, road back to the nest with arrow. S = Saucer.

over; instead, it looked for another route and chose the way to the right, around the bowl (Fig. 68, III). On its way back it again climbed over the bowl.

On its fourth sortie, the ant chose the road directly to the food (Fig. 69, IV), but on the way back it made a loop to the right and came upon the obstacle. Here it hesitated and then ran round it to the left (Fig. 69, IV). It did the same on several return journeys. Then with intermittent relapses, it began to change direction before actually reaching the obstacle, both on the outward and on the return trip (Fig. 70, VI and VII). In the end the ant avoided the bowl on every trip, and without a false start.

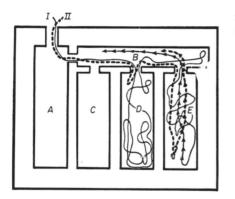

FIG. 71. Labyrinth for memory test.

In another experiment, we let *Messor* ants run into a labyrinth, shown in Fig. 71. In the lower end of Chamber D we placed fifteen carrot seeds and in Chamber E fifteen fennel seeds. The ants found the carrot seeds in the manner already known to us; the experiment became interesting only after the last of these had been dragged off. Now an ant began to look for more seeds in Chamber D. After searching in vain, it left the chamber and, after some wandering, reached the fennel seeds in Chamber E (Fig. 71, I). A seed was dragged off to the nest, and the ant appeared again in the frame, at first in Chamber D, which it searched carefully. After vain efforts the seeds in E were again discovered, and again a seed was hauled away.

This performance was repeated once again; but the third time, the ant went only a short way into Chamber D (Fig. 71, II). Then it turned about and went straight to Chamber E. We were eager to see whether the ant would retain a lasting memory of the new situation. At first it did not; it made two more trips to Chamber D. But it always noticed the mistake after a few steps and went no further into Chamber D, not even after a few new fennel seeds had been put there. Instead, it turned about and hurried to Chamber E, which it gradually emptied.

In this performance the *Messor* ants showed high mental capacities, not only in that they mastered a new situation, but also in their way of doing it. The repeated correction of mistakes pointed to a definite "intellectual" accomplishment.

Young ants, we have shown, undergo a certain schooling; they are not able to perform all of their tasks from the very first. In dealing with a food source or prey, the callows often show an awkwardness such as is never seen in older ants. On the other hand, young ants can accustom themselves to circumstances that throw their elders into great excitement; they learn, for example, to take continuous disturbances in artificial nests for granted. On several occasions we wished to set up several nests, but had only a single queen. Our solution was to let the queen spend a few days in each nest. In this way we averted the restlessness that always sets in after some time in a queenless nest. Besides, the queen laid a few eggs in each nest.

All the nests quickly grew used to the repeated disturbances. The workers remained quiet when we removed the queen, and after a while the queen herself ceased to offer the slightest resistance.

We have seen how ants adapt themselves to a trail that was made neither by themselves nor by others of their own species. The ants that made the trail also learn to accept that they are not the only users. At first they drive out the intruders; later, their resistance dwindles, and in the end they develop toleration. We have earlier described such a case of gradual habituation. The process seems to have been favored by the fact that one set of ants gradually took on something of the other's odor; the *Camponotus lateralis*, which borrowed the trail, are so close in color to the *Cremastogaster* that even ant collectors have confused the two species.

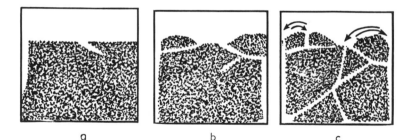

a   b   c

FIG. 72 *a-c*. Groups of the Chilean ant *Solenopsis gayi* working against each other in an artificial nest, as in Fig. 34. *a*) At the end of four hours the ants had built the beginnings of a nest in the earth between two glass plates; one shaft went vertically down the edge of the nest, another started from the middle and slanted down to the right. *b*) After another four hours a second entrance hole had been dug beside each of those already made. *c*) The ants busy in the new holes threw the earth back into the other holes where their companions were working. Despite this work at cross purposes, a proper crater nest in the manner of Fig. 26, containing broad chambers and passages, had been built by next day. To judge by the final result one would have said that the ants had been working according to a plan from the very start.

Very young ants grow accustomed to all sorts of novelties; older ones are less adaptable. If we take young and old ants from a colony in the open and put them together in an artificial nest, the outcome is almost always the same: next day we find a number of dead ants showing no trace of injury. There are deaths on the following days as well. It is always the older individuals that perish in this way, never the young. Like elderly human beings torn away from their accustomed surroundings, they cannot adapt themselves to the new situation. They grow restless and excitable, and die of excitement or a sudden "stroke."

The ant, then, can learn and adapt to new situations. But in regard to the higher psychical faculties we must bear this in mind: Even in its supreme accomplishments, an ant has no insight into the relations between ends and means, not to mention cause and effect. All attempts to demonstrate reason in ants have ended in utter failure.

For example: a strip of glass coated with honey is placed over an ant highway. The ants visit it eagerly. Now the disk is gradually raised until finally it is out of the ants' reach. They rear up on their hind legs and do their best to reach it. But they never hit on the idea of raising the ground, although in building their nests they are able to throw up earthworks with great rapidity.

All such experiments have yielded the same result. One of them is shown in Fig. 73. A platform is attached to one end of a stick or wire forming an acute angle. On this platform, which is only a small fraction of an inch above the ground, are placed some larvae. By raising themselves up on their hind legs, the ants on the ground (*Lasius niger*) can touch the larvae with their antennae; they cannot climb up on the platform. The result never varies: The ants make desperate efforts to reach the larvae, but it never occurs to them to pile up a few bits of earth under the edge of the platform and to climb up, though these adroit masons are perfectly capable of such an operation.

Lubbock Avebury, the well-known ant specialist to whom we owe this experiment, placed some ants on the plate with the larvae (Fig. 73 *d*) and trained them to return to their nest via *b* and *a*. Gradually they became familiar with the road and brought back companions with them; soon a whole team was busily transporting larvae. At first, the ants on the plate made desperate efforts to reach the ground with their larvae directly from the platform. They could see the ground, and even feel it with their antennae. But none of them ever thought of simply tossing the larvae down to avoid the repeated difficult journeys, although they must have had countless occasions to observe that such a slight fall does not injure larvae.

FIG. 73. Experiment for testing the intelligence of the garden ant *Lasius niger*.

All such tests showed that ants are lacking in any genuine reasoning power or understanding of cause and effect. This explains why we often see such absurdities as several teams of ants working against one another—of this Fig. 72 offers a fine example. Another absurdity is the rearing of enemy aliens whose larvae eat the brood of the ants. If we credited the ants with higher intelligence, ant biology would become a maze of hopeless contradictions: the surprising thing would be what the ants *cannot* do rather than what they *can* do.

To sum up our remarks on ant psychology. They are certainly not, as was formerly thought, "machines" reacting blindly to all outward stimuli, more or less in the manner of iron filings attracted or repelled by a magnet. This notion is refuted by the observed accomplishments of the ants, which show not only considerable memory and a gift for combining experiences, but also a distinct power of individual adaptation. On the other hand, they have no human reasoning power; if they did, certain absurdities in their social life would be inexplicable. In any event, the ant's brain is not equal to an insight into cause and effect.

But is the ant's brain, which in the smaller forms measures only a tiny fraction of a millimeter, the exclusive seat of its mental function?

On this point there can no longer be any doubt. An injury to the so-called pedunculate bodies (cf. Figs. 3 and 74) produces very much the same results as does an injury to the cerebrum in humans. An ant whose brain has been injured by the bite of another first remains motionless as though nailed to the spot—then a trembling runs through its whole body, and from time to time one of its legs shoots up in the air. In response to an irritation, it may continue to make defensive movements, but as soon as the stimulus ceases it falls back into its stupor. It is totally incapable of any purposeful action. It no longer attempts to run away, to attack, to return to its nest, or to join its mates; it no longer draws away from the sun, water, or cold. In short, it has completely lost the simplest instincts of self-preservation. An ant wounded in this way is in reality nothing but a "set of reflexes." According to the studies of Forel, celebrated brain specialist and myrmecologist, it fully resembles a vertebrate whose cerebrum has been injured or removed.

The mental faculties of ants may also be impaired in other ways. We encounter "insane" ants which behave very differently from the other members of the colony. They attack and bite their fellows until in the end the

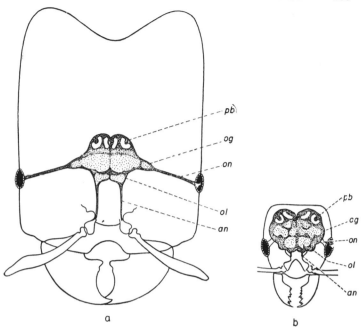

FIG. 74 *a-b*. Head of a soldier (*a*) and worker (*b*) of *Pheidole instabilis*. Despite its gigantic head the soldier has a brain no larger than that of the worker. pb = pedunculate bodies, which correspond to the cerebrum of the vertebrates; og = optic ganglion; on = optic nerve; ol = olfactory lobe; an = antennary nerve.

colony must do away with them. We once subjected one of these apparently mad ants to close observation, kept a case history, and after its death dissected the body. Its "cerebrum" was indeed diseased: we found a growth, a kind of tumor, which provoked mental disorders just as in man—a clear indication that the pedunculate bodies of the ant are the seat of its mental faculties.

In the male ant the "cerebrum" is usually atrophied; in the females it is well developed; and it is most fully developed in the workers (Fig. 3). The behavior of the three groups corresponds to their brain structure: the males may truly be called stupid, the females are far superior, and the highest faculties are those of the workers on whom depends the whole welfare of the state.

One would think that the soldiers with their larger heads possess larger brains than do the workers. But this is not the case. A comparison between Fig. 74 *a* and *b* shows there is little difference either in size or in structure. The immense skull lodges the soldier's large muscles which move the powerful jaws, but no larger brain—and indeed, the soldiers are not superior to the workers in the performance of their tasks.

The Origin of the Soldiers

This brings us back to the different castes and classes among ants. But now we shall consider this matter from a different angle. Instead of merely noting what these forms are, we shall ask why there are so many of them. This is a question of general biological interest, worth looking into. At the same time, we shall cast a glance into the myrmecologist's workshop.

In asking "why," a biologist cannot rely wholly on observation. He must perform experiments in the hope of demonstrating hypotheses which he may have formed on some other grounds.

Students of ants had long sought an explanation for the different forms of female ants. Some have thought that a predisposition to the different sizes and shapes was contained in the egg—and have spoken of a "blastogenic" origin. Others have seen the cause in the quantity or kind of the food—and have spoken of a "trophogenic" origin.

As far as the formation of soldiers is concerned, the veil has partly been lifted. In experiments with the Italian house ant (*Pheidole pallidula*, Fig. 7), it has been possible to produce soldiers at will, and even to construct forms halfway between workers and soldiers such as do not occur in nature.

These experiments show that there is some truth in each of the two hypotheses mentioned. It has become clear that not every egg can produce a soldier. A young queen, just fertilized by a male and proceeding to found a nest lays, we know, a number of eggs from which only tiny ants emerge. My colleagues and I have observed the founding of hundreds of such states in simple tubes (Fig. 65). The tiny workers that emerge from the first eggs are only a stopgap. They are not only small but short-lived, and in some species they die at the end of a few weeks. Even though she is well nourished, the first eggs of a young queen cannot be made to produce normal workers or normal soldiers. If we take the eggs from a colony that has already produced normal workers and soldiers, and substitute the eggs of a young queen, these will again yield only small workers. Thus, their formation is largely determined in the egg.

The later eggs of a queen, who by the appearance of the first small workers is relieved of the burden of caring for the eggs all by herself and is now better nourished than before, may yield either normal workers or soldiers; now food turns out to be the determining factor.

I noted that colonies enjoying a superior food supply furnished a larger number of soldiers than did others. This observation suggested various feeding experiments that we need not discuss in detail. As a rule, ant cultures were divided into two groups, approximately equal in population and quantity of brood. One group was fed for ten days exclusively on sugar water or honey, and the others on meat of insects; after ten days I changed the menus for fear that such unbalanced diets might cause deaths. I knew that at a temperature of approximately 75° Fahrenheit the egg stage, the larva stage, and the pupa stage of the *Pheidole* ants, with which we were working, each required roughly ten days. This made it possible to figure out which phase of development corresponded to a diet of meat or of sugar.

The experiments showed that soldiers appeared only when a meat diet was made available to the larvae. Other experiments carried on over a period of months confirmed the result.

Changes in diet produced particularly striking effects. When a culture which had been receiving meat and producing soldiers was shifted to a diet of sugar, it ceased to produce soldiers; nests switched from sugar to insect meat soon developed giant larvae which produced soldier pupae and ultimately soldiers. Such results could be obtained only in colonies containing larvae not over five days old. The older larvae, even if they were fed meat, all developed into workers.

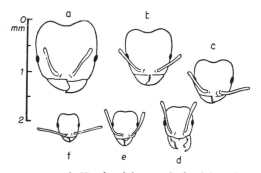

FIG. 75 *a-f.* Heads of forms of *Pheidole pallidula* which were intentionally produced in artificial nests. *a*) Normal soldier. *b*) Small soldier. *c*) Intermediate form. *d*) Large worker. *e*) Normal worker. *f*) Small worker. The forms *b* and *c* do not occur in nature. All the ants are descendants of the same queen ("Windsor" family, cf. Fig. 83).

To sum up: The experiments showed that if the larvae were fed plenty of insect meat during a certain sensitive or critical period (the second larval stage) they suddenly began to grow quickly and develop into soldiers; but if they were given no meat during this period they became workers. Later, it was discovered that insect meat, especially the dead termites used in the experiments, contains a special growth ingredient which caused the larvae's sudden increase in size. This substance was at

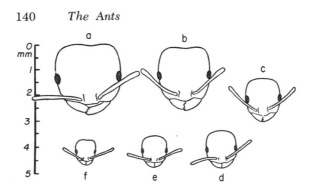

FIG. 76 *a-f*. Head forms of the harvester ant *Messor structor*, showing natural transitional form (*c*) intermediate between normal soldiers (*a*) and small soldiers (*b*) on the one hand, and large workers (*d*), normal workers (*e*), and small workers (*f*) on the other.

first called termitin. But when it was found in some of the lower fungi, for example the *Hypomyces* of the leaf-cutter ants, and in worms (*Tubifex*) and yeasts (*Torula*), it was given the name of T-complex or T-factor. This T-factor plays an important role in the life of other organisms, including man, by its power to awaken dormant reserves. Its effectiveness is particularly impressive in the development of soldier ants, which through it realize the potentiality present in the larvae.

Even after the caste has been determined at the beginning of the larval development, the size of the ants can still be affected by variations in diet. Although the normal forms are always preponderant, it is possible to produce in addition large workers and small soldiers (Fig. 75).

On several occasions we even succeeded in producing transitional forms between workers and soldiers by giving the colony a few bits of meat during the period of sugar diet and by disturbing the feeding larvae in various ways. The ant head shown in Fig. 75 *c* is 3.5 millimeters long, halfway between that of the normal worker, measuring 2.5 millimeters, and of the normal soldier, measuring 3.75 millimeters. This head may be regarded either as the end of the worker series or as the beginning of a soldier series.

Such transitional forms also occur in certain natural nests—we recall the harvesters of Fig. 9, and the fungus growers of Fig. 36. Some of the forms closely related to the house ants show such transitions but for this very

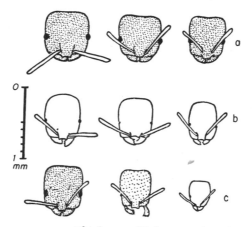

FIG. 77 *a-c.* Thief ant (*Solenopsis fugax*), heads from different nests. *a*) Top row: largest, intermediate, and smallest ants from a nest in Spain which contained only giants with large eyes (with spines at the end of the thorax). *b*) Second row: largest, intermediate, and smallest ants from a nest in Florence, Italy. All small, bright-colored, with etiolated eyes (without spines at the end of the thorax). *c*) Bottom row: large, medium, and small ants from an artificial nest in Breslau, Germany; the large individual corresponds completely to the inhabitants of nest *a*, the small one to those of *b*.

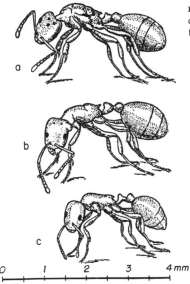

FIG. 78 *a-c.* *Leptothorax* species. *a*) Female. *b*) Transitional form. *c*) Worker.

0   1   2   3   4 mm

reason these ants are classified among different genera. What makes these transitional forms possible? Investigations have shown that these species have a much longer period of development than does the Italian house ant (*Pheidole pallidula*)—twice as long, for example, among the *Messor* harvesters. In consequence, chances of disturbance or change of diet are much greater. The larvae do not develop as quickly, and as a rule cannot feed undisturbed, and this accounts for the frequency of intermediate forms.

Similar conditions prevail among the thief ants (*Solenopsis fugax*, cf. Fig. 77), of which we shall have more to say, and apparently also among the fungus-growing species of South America, where we find every possible form of soldier and many forms of worker, but only seldom see intermediate forms that we hesitate to assign to either group.

The large soldiers seem to have much in common with the authentic females; the brain proportions of the very large forms, or giants as they are sometimes called, resemble those of the queen, and there is also a resemblance in the germ glands and organs of sight (cf. Fig. 36). Some species that possess only large workers, such as the very primitive *Ponera* species, have all sorts of intermediate forms between workers and authentic females. The *Leptothorax* species, which lives chiefly in oaks and other thick-barked trees, often has shown transitional forms between workers and authentic females (Fig. 78). Recent experiments with these species have given us some idea of what determines the development of a queen. Apparently, all favorable circumstances must coincide: Only the eggs of a female at the height of her development, who at the most favorable time of year and under the best environmental conditions has received a varied diet including vitamins and growth-promoting substances, seem to produce genuine long-lived females that contrast in every way with the first small, short-lived workers produced under the most unfavorable circumstances.

Sex

How do the males come into being? Here, too, ant specialists are now in agreement.

To an extent, our views of this aspect of ant biology are based on analogy with the bees which have been more thoroughly investigated. Among the bees, too, there is a queen who in her youth is only once fertilized by a male, in a "nuptial flight" similar to that of the ants. Like the ant queen, she carries the seed of her long-dead "prince consort" around for years thereafter in a special little sac in her abdomen. By a special apparatus she can transfer spermatozoa to the eggs as they pass by the sac. If she does so, the egg is fertilized, and fertilized eggs always produce females: a queen or a worker. If spermatozoa do not enter the egg, males (what among the bees are known as drones) are always the result. These processes have been studied in detail under the microscope.

All indications are that among the ants, which are closely related to the bees, sex is determined in the same way. Eggs are often laid by workers or even soldiers, which, as we have seen, are very close to being authentic females. With rare exceptions such eggs produce only males. Unable to rise into the air in marriage flights, workers and soldiers remain unfertilized. Yet the eggs of some workers have become genuine females. The explanation is that in their nuptial frenzy the males often approach females on the ground or in the nest and on such occasions may fertilize a worker by mistake. I myself have seen this happen. Such workers may, on very exceptional occasions, lay fertilized eggs that produce females. If workers are raised from larvae and pupae in artificial nests and never brought into contact with males, their eggs—definitely unfertilized—never produce anything but males.

It was more difficult to perform the same experiment with definitely unfertilized queens. Workers without a queen can be kept in artificial nests such as that shown in Fig. 66, but an unfertilized queen usually sickens after a short time. The life of an "old maid" is normal for the workers, but not for her. Even if she does lay eggs, she cannot tend them. But we did at last succeed with a *Leptothorax* ant, and managed to carry out our experiment. The segregated females laid and tended eggs, but only males issued from them since they were unfertilized. Here we have another strong indication that among the ants, as among the bees, males issue from unfertilized eggs.

I should stress that this form of sex determination is by no means universal, but an exception apparently limited to the bees, the ants, and a few other social insects.

Body Form and Heredity

The development of soldiers and workers is conditioned by their environment; which of the two forms is produced depends on the quantity and kind of food they get in a given phase of development. The length of the period of development also plays a part; the longer it is, the greater the likelihood of disturbances or of changes of diet that may bring about all sorts of intermediate forms.

The period of development varies with the species. Among the *Pheidole*, we have seen, it is very short; the whole development from egg to ant takes barely a month. For other ants it is much longer. The black carpenter ant (*Camponotus herculaneus*), for example, showed the following periods: from egg to larva, 16 to 27 days; from larva to pupa, 8 to 15 days; and from pupa to worker, 14 to 92 days. Among the common small garden ants (*Lasius*), which have been observed extensively, the egg stage required 13 to 30 days; the larval stage 9 to 24 days; and the pupal stage 16 to 36 days. The corresponding periods for the subterranean yellow ant (*Lasius flavus*) are 22 to 52, 7 to 31, and 16 to 49 days; for the Argentine ant (*Iridomyrmex humilis*), 11 to 20, 8 to 29, and 8 to 35 days.

The wide spread between the two figures given for each phase is due to the fact that the cultures we observed were kept at different temperatures, the second figure corresponding to the temperatures prevailing in

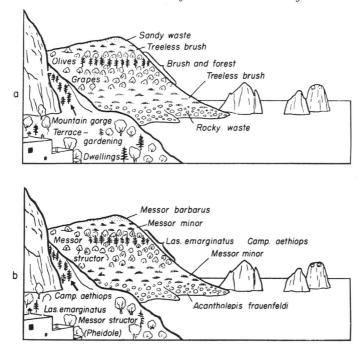

FIG. 79 *a-b. a*) Punta Tragara in Capri with its various wild and cultivated zones. *b*) A particular ant species predominates in each zone.

our latitudes. The first figure gives the periods of development for cultures kept at a steady temperature of 79° to 86°.

Do these experiments have any bearing on our problem, the origin of workers and soldiers? No, not directly. But they do point to certain more general considerations. We have mentioned that the occurrence of soldiers is thought to be a distinguishing characteristic of the *Pheidole* ants, while the presence of numerous transitional forms between the largest and the smallest workers is considered one of the features of the *Messor* spe-

cies. We have also seen that the intermediate forms do
not occur among the *Pheidole* species only because the
larvae develop quickly. The distinguishing characteristic
would seem to be the rate of development. But since this
rate of development can be influenced artificially, it can
no longer be regarded as the distinguishing characteristic, but merely as a feature of the genus which, within
certain limits, can be modified by the environment.

Our earth, now, shows the widest variety of environmental conditions, and a wide variety of ant species.
Every clearly defined region—forest, desert, steppe, and
so on—harbors definite forms of ants (cf. Figs. 79 and
80), which, as we have seen, may differ widely in the
kind of dwelling they live in, and the kinds of food they
eat. They resemble the ants of similar regions but different climates, and yet are often enough unlike them to
be designated as different subspecies or races (geo-
graphical and ecological races). If on different parts of
the earth we were to find forms of ants that differ from
one another as greatly as the *Pheidole* workers differ
from the *Pheidole* soldiers, we should surely take them
for distinct species, perhaps even for members of different genera. It is only because we know that *Pheidole*
workers and soldiers come from the same parents that
we regard them as members of the same species.

Two sister queens of some suitable species might
very well find their way to radically different localities: one to a warm area with abundant food at the
critical period when diet can induce the formation of
soldiers, and the other to a cool, barren place where these
decisive factors are always absent. A collector lacking
in imagination would be sure to identify them as two
different species, particularly in view of the huge population of every single nest.

This thought is not a mere flight of fancy. Chile in particular lends itself to such observations (Fig. 80). The

country consists of a long, thin strip of land extending
from the torrid zone to the Antarctic, and has a great diversity of climates. The land rises from sea level to alti-
tudes of 21,000 feet, so that even at identical latitudes we
find widely varying conditions. Thus, queens of the same
species may after their nuptial flight make their nests in
very different regions. A queen from the warm low-lying
plain may be wafted to the edge of icy volcanoes, another
may be borne from the hot desert to cool damp forests,
or vice versa. I have frequently noted such occurrences.

The colonies established by some of these ants showed
striking variations according to climate and food supply.
In the desert regions of Chile the *Pogonomyrmex* har-

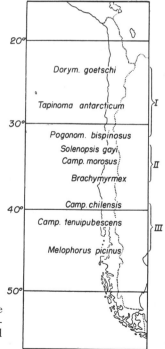

FIG. 80. Map of Chile showing the
centers of distribution of the Chilean desert (I), steppe (II), and
wood (III) ants.

vesters, which in other localities present a variety of forms (for example, *P. barbatus,* with workers measuring five to nine millimeters long), were represented by colonies consisting solely of soldiers or giants (*P. bispinosus*), while in the jungle (*P. laevigatus*) they showed no distinct soldier caste. My observations at the time showed that both in natural and in artificial nests *P. bispinosus* always feeds its young on solid food, ant bread or bits of insects, while *P. laevigatus* does not. I also found that the steppe ant *Solenopsis gayi,* which in northern and central Chile ate seeds in addition to its liquid food, dispensed with grain in the forests of the south. Accordingly, its colonies, which in the north contained varied types, often including immense giants, were more homogeneous and without giants in the south. Experiments with the closely related thief ant (*Solenopsis fugax*) completed these findings and showed that the *Solenopsis* species react strongly to outward conditions. The enormous colonies of these ants usually contain individuals varying widely in color and size. They range from small, light-colored individuals with tiny visual organs to large, dark ones with well-developed eyes (Fig. 77 *c*). Some colonies are quite uniform, as is shown by a comparison between Fig. 77 *a* and *b*. Ants of the nest exemplified in Fig. 77 *a* consisted of giants only, with square skulls, further distinguished by strong spines on the end of the thorax, large eyes, and dark color, like the giants of other species. The ants of the nest exemplified in Fig. 77 *b* contained no distinct giants, its members were light yellow, with tiny eyes, and without spines of any kind. The two colonies were different enough to be set down as different species. But it proved possible to transform a colony of small light-colored ants into one with predominantly large dark ones—the favorable conditions prevailing in captivity allowed nearly all of the young larvae

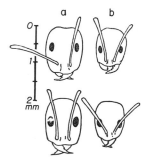

FIG. 81 *a-b.* Heads of Chilean desert ants (*Dorymyrmex goetschi*); workers from nests in different regions: *a*) Copiapó, latitude 30°, northern Chile; workers large. *b*) Punta Colorado, latitude 29°, a little to the south; workers small. The workers from one and the same nest are almost identical. ("Monomorphism" of the worker caste in contrast to "dimorphism," Figs. 7, 8, and 74 and "polymorphism," Figs. 10, 17, 36, and 76).

to develop into large ants. Thus, one "race" was by experiment transformed into another.

Even ant colonies with uniform population seem capable of developing different races in this way. The wood ants of Chile grow smaller toward the dry, barren north, the desert ants grow smaller in the cool steppes and woods to the south (Fig. 81). Every form has its own special region suited to it, and deteriorates in warmer, cooler, wetter, or drier conditions. This deterioration shows in its smaller size.

These findings are supported by experiment. The German garden ant (*Lasius niger*) is found as far to the south as central Italy. However, the Capri specimens, which occur only in cool, damp spots on Monte Solaro, are appreciably smaller than those from central Germany. The reverse applies to a close relative, *Lasius emarginatus*, which replaces *niger* in the warmer parts of Italy but ranges into Germany (Fig. 82). Breeding experiments carried out with the Italian garden ant under varying conditions showed that individuals growing up in a warm place attain larger sizes than do those kept at lower temperatures. As Fig. 82 shows, this accords with observations in nature: an ant from a Silesian nest in Annaberg grew to be barely as large as the forms raised

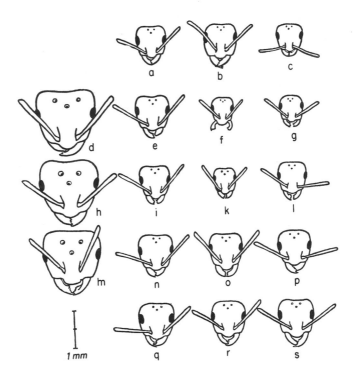

FIG. 82 *a-s*. Effect of outward influences, such as climate or breeding conditions (= normal modifications), on the size of the Italian garden ant (*Lasius emarginatus*), which in the south replaces the German garden ant (*Lasius niger*). Heads of different individuals from different regions and with different breeding conditions. *a*) Worker from Palermo, somewhat smaller than normal. *b*) Worker of normal size from the Galli Islands. *c*) Worker from St. Annaberg, Upper Silesia; small, corresponds to g bred in low temperature. *d*) Queen from nest CB₄, Bagni di Tiberio, Capri, sister of worker e and mother of f (= first worker) and g (= normal worker bred at low temperature). *e*) Worker from nest CB₄, Bagni di Tiberio, Capri, sister of queen d, "aunt" of f and g. *f*) First worker of queen d, sister of normal worker g, born later and raised at low temperature. *g*) Normal worker of queen d, bred at low temperature, sister of first worker f, corresponds in

in the cold artificial nest (Fig. 82 *c* and *g*), while the individuals bred in Germany at temperatures of 75° to 83° resembled the forms from Capri (Fig. 82 *l* and *i*). The most favorable temperature has an upper limit; ants in Palermo, where it gets still hotter than in Capri, are often smaller, like colonies of German ants in Italy.

In interpreting such observations, of course, take account of all other relevant circumstances as well. The Carinthian forms of *Lasius emarginatus*, for example, are relatively large (Fig. 82 *m-p*). But this colony, under observation for twenty years, inhabits a house and is kept warm in winter. The ants stay indoors even in spring and fall. Luckily for them, the house belongs to a zoologist who is interested in ants.

The Italian harvester ants, as we have seen, turn out large or small according to conditions. As we go north from southern Italy (Naples), both the nest population and size of *Messor structor* decrease. At the foot of the Alps, the workers measure only 1½ to 1⅔ compared with 3 to 3½ millimeters in the south. All these ants feed on grain, and accordingly each colony shows a diversity of forms. Because of the less favorable climate the giants of the north measure only 4 to 5 millimeters, compared with the 9 to 10 millimeters of their southern kin. There

size to the Silesian *c*. *h*) Queen of nest CB, Bagni di Tiberio, Capri, sister of worker i, mother of first worker k and of the normal worker l, bred at high temperature. *i*) Worker of nest CB, Bagni di Tiberio, Capri, sister of queen h, "aunt" of k and l. *k*) First worker of queen h, sister of the normal worker l, bred later. *l*) Normal worker of queen h, bred at high temperature and corresponding in size to the normal individuals of the Galli Islands (b) and Capri (i). *m*) Female from the Krumpendorf nest (in a house), Carinthia, sister of n, o, and p. *n, o, p*) Normal workers of the Krumpendorf nest, Carinthia, from the years 1932 (n), 1935 (o), and 1936 (p). This colony, observed over a period of 20 years, always provided individuals of the same size, which always grew up under favorable conditions (in a house heated in winter). *q*) Normal worker from Brixen in the South Tyrol. *r*) Normal worker from Lugano. *s*) Normal worker from Torbole.

is also a difference in the queens, though here our figures are not yet sufficient to make comparisons.

We have also been able to breed males of various sizes. The differences in size between northern and southern members of the species are often so great as to make mating between them impossible—just as a sheep dog cannot mate with a dachshund. They are then well on their way to constituting different races.

Similar developments have been found among other groups of animals.

Another important factor determining body forms which we must not neglect is heredity, which we study in the science of genetics. The *Pheidole* ants, for example, show genuine "hereditary" or Mendelian races, in addition to the forms caused by the influences of their environment. Anyone who, like myself, observes a number of pure-bred families for any length of time gets to know his strains as well as any shepherd or cattle breeder. It is unthinkable that I should confuse members of the "Windsor" family with those of the "Tiberio" or "Tragara" families. Other strains, too, with less poetic names have been analyzed so closely that they cannot possibly be confused (Fig. 83). Among the *Pheidole* ants, the differences in size and coloration (in the "Windsor" family, for example, a black spot on the relatively light-colored head) or in biological behavior, may be so pronounced that they warrant speaking of different species or at least subspecies. There is no doubt that ants, like domestic animals, present color races. This is particularly evident in investigations based on several successive generations, as was the case with the "Windsor" family. I was well acquainted with their queen from the moment she left her nest, and was able to examine her less fortunate sisters, that is, the workers and soldiers of this nest, and the male, her "prince consort." On careful examination of the

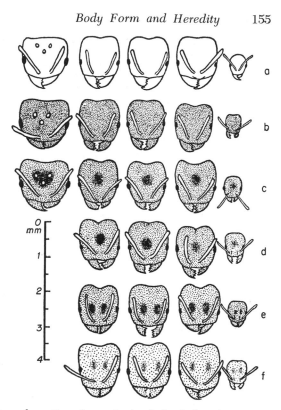

FIG. 83 *a-f*. Race formation (mutation) of the Italian house ant *Pheidole pallidula*. At left, females with frontal eyes; in the center, three soldiers; at right, a worker. Each horizontal row comes from one nest. *a*) San Alessandro, Ischia, base color yellow, head without spots. *b*) Solaro G 8, Capri, base color dark brown. *c*) Windsor C 15, Capri, base color brown, head with one spot. *d*) Windsor F I, Capri, base color brown, one spot on head. (The members of this colony are the "siblings" of the queen of Windsor C 15 above; the two generations show conspicuous agreement in color and markings. *e*) Tiberio B 25, Capri, base color brown, two spots on head. *f*) San Romualdo P. 44, Rovigno, base color light brown, suggestion of two spots on head.

Identical coloration of horizontal rows is brought about by hereditary mutations, the identical form of the vertical rows by similar diet at certain critical or sensitive periods.

forms the points of resemblance between blood kin were evident (cf. Fig. 83 *c* and *d*).

Thus, environmental and hereditary factors combine. Workers and soldiers, totally different in body form, bear the badge of like heredity: one or two black spots in the middle of the forehead, darker or lighter general coloration, and other features. Despite her entirely different body form, the queen—their common mother—shows the same features. We begin to see why the ants represent so complex a problem for systematic zoology.

The Seasonal Rhythm

Among the "race" characteristics we must also count certain inner processes that present something of a puzzle. We cannot always be quite sure whether they are hereditary or stem from environmental modifications that have become more or less stabilized. I am thinking principally of the seasonal rhythms.

We take for granted that trees sprout leaves in the spring and shed them in the fall. These processes are commonly attributed to outward conditions—the warmer weather in March, the cooler weather in November—and indeed there is some truth to this opinion. The same holds for the animals which grow heavy fur in winter and molt at the beginning of summer.

But if we transfer plants and animals with such annual rhythms to the Southern Hemisphere where the seasons are reversed—where Christmas is celebrated in midsummer and our summer solstice falls in midwinter—we soon find out that the growth of leaves and fur is not clearly dependent on environment.

For example: A shipment of camels from Hamburg, Germany, arrived at the zoo at Santiago, Chile. They had started their journey in the autumn of the Northern Hemisphere, and arrived in the Southern Hemisphere with their heavy winter coats. They kept these coats all through the summer which in Santiago can be very hot. At the start of the southern winter, which in Santiago is often accompanied by snow and ice, they shed their wool in thick mats. In September, with the returning warmth of spring, their wool began to grow again!

Trees often behave in the same way. But there is usually a certain process of adaptation, favored by the fact that in southern Chile, as in many subtropical regions, plant growth is suspended twice yearly, rather than just once as in our latitudes: the vital processes are inhibited by the summer drought as well as by the cold rainy season. Some trees which in our climate begin to bloom in March after the winter pause, retained the habit in Santiago; they grew blossoms in March. But in Chile, it must be remembered, the reawakening followed the *summer* pause of January and February. Others, however, gradually adapted themselves to the Southern Hemisphere.

Certain vital processes, then, follow the rhythm of the annual cycle. They are subject to modification, but only within certain limits. This is true of plants as well as animals, and similar rhythms may be observed in collective organisms such as the ant societies.

In our latitudes, ant colonies make their appearance with the coming of spring. An ant appears outside the nest, which has often fallen into disrepair during the winter. Soon the first ant is joined by others, and they proceed at once to repair the damage and to gather food for the gradually awakening colony.

The queen at this time resumes her egg laying. The larvae that issue from these eggs, and the brood that has hibernated through the winter and now resumes its growth, must be fed; this keeps the workers busy. The pupae that have hibernated begin to turn into ants, and soon there are numerous young workers that begin at once to work zealously for the steadily increasing brood. As the season advances and the weather grows warmer, the queen, whose ovaries often swell enormously in the late spring, lays more and more eggs. The older workers, relieved of their domestic duties by the young ones, now busy themselves almost exclusively outside the nest, gathering food and building material. The colony spreads out and extends its sphere of influence.

Young ants emerge. Little by little the character of the population changes. When the queen started laying eggs, nurses were few and the brood large; one nurse may have as many as six to ten eggs or larvae to care for. Gradually, this relation is reversed. For some species of ants, the rate of egg production, and the length of different stages of development, allow us to compute the time when there will be a number of nurses for each larva. This is probably the moment when some of the best-cared-for larvae, fed on plenty of their nurses' saliva and other food rich in vitamins, develop into full females. They may benefit either directly, from the abundance of food received in the larval stage, or indirectly, through the queen who seems to produce the strongest offspring at this time. The warm weather also favors these processes, and when conditions are most favorable, even some of the workers lay eggs. These and some of the queen's eggs, which now are so abundant that some of them remain unfertilized, produce males. All this leads to the marriage flight, which takes place in the summer, earlier or later according to the species and its rate of development.

The annual cycle has reached its climax. The weather grows cooler, and the queen's egg production dwindles. Most of those workers that lived through the preceding winter have died, and many of the young ants born in the spring have met a natural end or have fallen victim to some catastrophe. Life grows quieter, and the colony begins to prepare for winter. When really cold weather sets in, the whole population retires deep into the earth. The adult ants fall into a kind of winter sleep, the brood's development is wholly suspended. Only the coming of spring awakens the colony to renewed activity.

This, by and large, is the annual cycle of the ants. There are considerable variations in detail. Some species develop more slowly, and their climax and nuptial flight do not occur until the late fall. In others, even the larvae or pupae of the sexed individuals hibernate, to complete their development in the early spring. Within one and the same species, the date of climax and marriage flight varies with the climate.

In the tropics and subtropics, the annual cycle of ant life is somewhat different. Development is inhibited by summer heat and drought as well as by winter coolness or rain. The steppe ants of both hemispheres have two climaxes and two rest periods—these, however, are not usually as distinct as in our latitudes. During these periods the many different species of harvesters seem at rest, but they are not asleep; they are feeding on provisions assembled in the spring or fall. The same holds true of the species that have developed honeypots and other storage devices (cf. Figs. 29–31). Their workers seldom live more than ten to twelve months, whereas in our latitudes, with their long periods of deep sleep, worker ants can live much more than a year. Among the harvesters, the two annual periods of growth and decline always produce two age groups among the workers: those born in the spring act as nurses during that season and in the fall engage in outside labors, while the opposite is true of those born in the autumn. Such ants have two marriage flights, though one or the other may be more important. When these species venture too far into colder regions, their rhythm may approach that prevailing in our latitudes. A case in point are the *Messor* species of northern Italy and the *Solenopsis* species of southern Chile, both of which have their principal habitat in warmer climates.

This annual rhythm is so firmly ingrained that it cannot be materially altered by experiment, though some changes can be brought about by application of unnatural cold or warmth. An increase of temperature can so accelerate the development of the German garden ant (*Lasius niger*), for example, that its cycle coincides with that of its southern cousin (*Lasius emarginatus*). Experiments with northern and southern carpenter ants have yielded similar results. But such artificial shifts do not agree with the animals for long, nor can we induce any real change in their life rhythm. Even if the nests of our indigenous ants are kept warm from fall to spring, they will start a rest period with the coming of winter. Even in laboratory cultures, kept at a uniform temperature throughout the year, sexed individuals appear at approximately the same time as they do in nature.

Ant societies, then, have their fixed annual rhythm. It can be changed artificially only within very narrow limits. This is why every species cannot live permanently in every climate any more than can the races of man.

Our discussion of the annual cycle and its effect on the ant society has thus led us to consider the general fate of ant genera and ant races. Similar problems are raised by the study of individuals whose fate, too, may be shaped by the seasons of the year. I am not talking of the accidents of fate—a shorter or longer life with this activity or that—but of the fate that is inevitably determined by the very structure of the animal.

We have stressed repeatedly that one and the same egg may produce an ant of any of the various castes and classes: An egg that is not fertilized when it leaves the body of its mother inevitably develops into a short-lived male. A male ant can fulfill its destiny only if it is big and strong; whether it will be big and strong depends largely on its food or, ultimately, on the season of its birth. If the egg has been fertilized it will turn, we know, into a female—but what kind of female depends mostly on the time the egg was laid. Only eggs whose larvae emerge during the most favorable season can turn into full-fledged females and future queens of a new colony. All other eggs furnish nothing but the mass of the population —the workers.

Again, there remain two possibilities. Among the species that possess soldiers, a larva must receive special food rich in protein and certain vitamins if it is to become a soldier. This can happen only at certain times of the year. If the larva does not develop during the favorable months when such a diet is available, it cannot become a soldier but will only be a worker.

Only a worker? Is it correct to speak in this way? Or should we not say that the period which we have just referred to as "favorable" constitutes a danger for the later development of the individual as well as the species? We cannot dispel such thoughts when we consider some of the outlandish soldier types that occur in many species of ants (Fig. 84 *d-f*). The sometimes enormous mandibles appearing in the *Pheidole* and *Messor* soldiers are outclassed by those of certain other soldiers. Such jaws are incapable of normal use, and many of these soldiers cannot even eat unaided. If they are not fed by others, they die. Such proportions are of no advantage to the individual, and they may easily make him a burden to the community. The jaws of the most extreme forms of soldiers cannot even bite; even for military purposes they are useless. A rich ant colony can afford to feed such monsters that contribute next to nothing; they do no lasting harm, for they cannot multiply and so injure the strain or species. But when hard times set in, the soldiers, as all observations show, are the first to succumb; in natural *Pheidole* nests, for example, they are the ones that perish with the coming of winter. They are the victims of the hyperorganization that impedes them in procuring food.

This brings us to the history of animals in general, for extreme forms of this kind are known to have died out among other families. In the course of the earth's history similar developments have led to the total extinction of certain species. The giant deer with antlers that were almost too heavy for them to carry and the mammoths with their great tusks invite comparison with the giant-headed ant soldiers.

I do not wish to be misunderstood: not all antlers and not all tusks are a drawback to the deer or elephant; on the contrary, they are usually very useful weapons. And the powerful jaws of the ant soldiers usually represent a

FIG. 84 *a-f.* Heads of soldiers. *a*) *Camponotus cognotus.* *b*) *Colobopsis impressa.* *c*) *Cheliomyrmex nortoni.* *d*) *Pheidole lamira.* *e*) *Harpegnathus cruentatus.* *f*) *Eciton hamatum.*

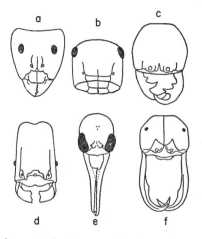

great advantage to the colony. In both cases the harm lies in exaggeration—a frequent tendency in overdeveloped organs. We all know that such exaggerated organs are impractical and that the animals possessing them succumb to better-adapted species. But biologists have often wondered why such impractical organs should have developed in the first place.

What we have learned about the development of *Pheidole* soldiers may give us some explanation. We have seen that they come into being only when a favorable situation prevails during a definite, brief period in the development of the brood. But in view of what we now know might we not do better to call this "favorable situation" a "danger factor"? Perhaps there were danger factors of this sort in the life of the extinct animals; perhaps these danger factors became operative only with a change in climate that accelerated or slowed down the process of gestation.

Experiments with the *Lasius* ants show that the life cycle can be speeded up by an increase in temperature, and the artificial breeding of giants among the *Messor* and *Pheidole* species indicates that formative factors of the kind we have been discussing can become decisive when the rate of development is accelerated.

Slowly but surely our observation of ant life has brought us to fundamental questions of biology. This need not surprise us. Nature is an inseparable whole; if we look closely enough at any part of it, we always come to fundamental problems. And in the end we shall find some connection between the animals and ourselves—for we ourselves are more a part of nature than we usually realize. It should not surprise us that in observing the ant societies we always find reminders of ourselves and our own societies, but the ants have found the solution to a problem with which we humans are still struggling.

The vertebrates—amphibians and reptiles, birds, and mammals—are assuredly the most successful members of the animal world. In various ways they have established superiority over the other animals, which they outdo in size, weight, and longevity. Their body structure and economy makes them the most efficient members of the animal world. Among the animal groups they have been eminently successful in the struggle for existence. They have gained more and more ground; today every part of the earth is dominated by the vertebrates. With one exception they are without serious competitors.

The social insects are the exception. By their tight social organization they have managed to compensate for the small stature that makes them seem inferior to the vertebrates. The result is that the vertebrates, up to and including man, still have to struggle with the societies of the ants and termites. But once a vertebrate, armed with all his superiority, began to do what the insects had done —once it began to set up societies to which the individual was to a certain extent subordinated—it was inevitable, from a purely biological point of view, that such a being should come to dominate not only the insects but the other vertebrates as well.

This is just what has happened. Man, with his physical superiority as an individual, took this step and became the lord of all living creatures. Yet man has retained far more individuality than the insects, and consequently his social life is not without its frictions. The states of men, like the colonies of ants, remain markedly hostile to one another. Let us hope that man, whose reason is far superior to the mental capacities of the ants, will gradually come to realize that friendship is more useful to him than enmity; let us hope that in this respect as in others man will rise above the ants!

Appendix: Termites ("White Ants")

Even the educated layman often regards termites as a kind of large ant. This view is incorrect. Termites are not ants in the biological sense, and are as far removed from ants in the system of animal life as an elephant is from a camel.

FIG. 85 *a-b*. *a*) Soldier. *b*) Grown larva (pseudo-worker) of the Mediterranean termite *Kalotermes flavicollis*. In the *Kalotermes* species the grown larvae have the function of workers; after passing through nymphal stages they can develop into winged males and females, the future kings and queens of the termite colony. The soldiers, which like the pseudo-workers may be either male or female, have completed their development; they never grow wings.

There are differences in body form: unlike the ants the termites have no waist between thorax and abdomen (Figs. 1, 4, and 9). The ant larva is a legless grub (Fig.

5 *a*), while the termite larva has six legs like an adult. And the termite society differs very considerably from that of the ants. For the greater part of the year the ants' nest is an "Amazonian" state. Like drones in a beehive, the males are present only during brief periods and have no other purpose than to fertilize the queen. A termite nest includes as many males as females: there is a king as well as a queen, and the workers and soldiers—for the termites too have soldiers—may be either male or female. But a superficial resemblance in the appearance and habits of the two families led to the idea that they were the same. Termites are called white ants in most of the world's principal languages.

Suggested Readings

AVEBURY, JOHN LUBBOCK
  Ants, Bees, and Wasps. London, 1898.

BUCKINGHAM, EDITH N.
  Division of Labor Among Ants. London, 1911.

DONISTHORPE, HORACE
  British Ants. London, 1927.
  Guests of the British Ants. London, 1928.

FOREL, AUGUSTE
  The Social World of the Ants. London, 1927.

MC COOK, HENRY C.
  Ant Communities and How They Are Governed. New
  York and London, 1909.

MOGGERIDGE, TRAHERNE
  Harvesting Ants and Trapdoor Spiders. London, 1873.

MORLEY, DEREK W.
  The Ant World. London, n.d.
  The Evolution of an Insect Society. London, 1954.

REAUMUR, RENÉ A. F. DE
  The Natural History of Ants. Tr. by W. M. Wheeler.
  New York, 1926.

SCHNEIRLA, T. C.
  Learning and Orientation in Ants Studied by Means of
  the Maze Method. Baltimore, 1929.

TURNER, CHARLES H.
  The Homing of Ants. Chicago, 1907.

WASMANN, ERIC

Psychology of the Ants and of the Higher Animals. London, 1905.

WEBER, N. A.

Observations on Baghdad Ants. Baghdad, 1952.

WHEELER, WILLIAM MORTON

Ants. New York, 1910.

Colony-founding Among Ants. Cambridge, Mass., 1933.

Mosaics and Other Anomalies Among Ants. Cambridge, Mass., 1937.

The Social Insects. New York, n.d.

INDEX